BEYOND THE CELTIC CROSS

Secret techniques for taking Tarot to an exciting new level

PAUL HUGHES-BARLOW
AND CATHERINE CHAPMAN

First published in 2009 by
Aeon Books Ltd.
London W5
www.aeonbooks.co.uk

Copyright © Paul Hughes-Barlow & Catherine Chapman 2009
The rights of Paul Hughes-Barlow and Catherine Chapman to be identified as the sole authors of this work have been asserted in accordance with §§ 77 and 78 of the Copyright Design and Patents Act 1988.

All rights reserved. No part of this publication may be reproduced, stored in a retrieval system, or transmitted, in any form or by any means, electronic, mechanical, photocopying, recording, or otherwise, without the prior written permission of the publisher.

British Library Cataloguing in Publication Data
A C.I.P. is available for this book from the British Library.

ISBN-13: 978-1-9046-583-44

Contents

Acknowledgements	v
Foreword by Douglas Gibb	vii
Introduction	1
The Celtic Cross Spread	9
Learning To Card Count	25
Understanding The Four Elements	45
Changing The Dynamics	51
The Rules Of Elemental Dignities	61
Pairing The Cards	69
Analysing Three-Card Combinations	77
Advanced Elemental Analysis And Elemental Bases	87
The Transforming Power Of The Aces	101
Uncounted Cards: The Magic Of Tarot	107
Who Is The Knight Of Wands?	115
Catherine's Vision	119
Epilogue	125
About The Authors	129

Acknowledgements

My thanks in particular go to Jackie O'Neal for her patience and tolerance, encouragement, insights and suggestions, and proof-reading skills throughout this project.

Paul Hughes-Barlow

The road hasn't always been smooth, but the ride has been made a lot easier by the love and support of my family and friends who have walked alongside me on this path. They're a very special bunch and I love them all. Special mentions go to my father, John Chapman, who continues to be my champion, supporter and inspiration; to Douglas Gibb who continues to encourage me, and without whose input and support my website *Tarot Elements* wouldn't exist; and to Helen Edwards because her faith can move mountains and her faith in me never faltered—she was so often my guinea pig throughout this whole process; and last but certainly not least, to Paul Hughes-Barlow—thank you for everything, the journey has been immense and I know it continues on.

Catherine Chapman

Foreword by Douglas Gibb

Paul and Catherine's book is a truly unique and innovative approach to the Celtic Cross Spread. They take the reader on a remarkable journey that starts with the Celtic Cross Spread in its traditional 'positional based' layout and, during the course of the book, transform it into a linear based spread.

This journey includes the use of techniques that were originally developed for the Opening of the Key Spread and chronicles Catherine's own Spiritual journey, culminating in a series of powerful initiating visions.

In my professional Tarot practice, I use the Opening of the Key Spread for face-to-face clients, but tend to shy away from using it when conducting telephone readings. However, this book provides the perfect solution. I now use the Celtic Cross Spread as a linear based system, which allows me to implement the techniques normally applied to the Opening of the Key Spread. I've found that Paul and Catherine's innovative approach to the Tarot has benefited not only myself as a Professional Tarot reader, but also my telephone-based clients as well.

One of the unique features of this book is the dialogue between Paul and Catherine. Paul is a guide, while Catherine examines and interprets the cards in great detail. It's clear that both of them learn a great deal from each other, and, each in their own manner, their understanding is enriched by the process.

The transforming experience that unfolds from the application of these techniques will benefit the reader in many subtle ways, on both a practical and a spiritual level.

Douglas Gibb
Professional Tarot Reader
http://taroteon.com

INTRODUCTION

Have you ever wondered how you can bring greater depth and clarity to your tarot readings? Have you struggled to understand just what exactly is going on in a reading and how the cards relate to its object?

For the first time, I'm going to show you how the professionals use secret techniques that take tarot readings to new and exciting levels. We will go beyond the surface levels of the Tarot spread and explore hidden gems. Have you ever wondered why some parts of the reading make no sense to you or your client? Have you found yourself going around in circles in a reading? Have you felt 'stuck'? What do you do when the final outcome card is the Ten of Swords or Death or some other 'difficult' card? I will show you how to overcome all these problems and more.

To do this, we shall analyse an actual tarot reading that was emailed to me by Catherine Chapman. She was having problems understanding it, particularly two Knights that appeared in the future positions. Together, over a period of ten days, we uncovered the tools and methods needed to transform the reading.

Catherine had used the Celtic Cross spread. Here are what the positions of the cards signified within that spread:

1. Heart of the Matter
2. Opposing Factor
3. Root Cause
4. Past
5. Attitudes & Beliefs
6. Future
7. You As You Are
8. Outside Environment
9. Hopes & Fears
10. Outcome

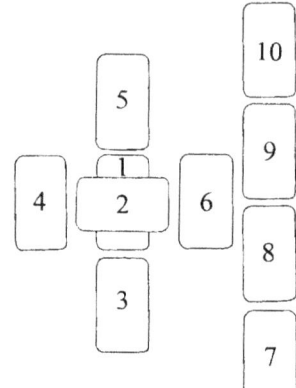

There are many variations on the Celtic Cross spread, but this does not make much difference once we have gone below the surface of the reading to explore its hidden depths. As we study the cards in the reading, I recommend that you have them laid out in front of you. Use a tarot deck you are familiar with. As you will come to see, the divinatory meanings of the cards are not as important as you might expect. If you have learnt the divinatory meaning of the positions differently from those described above, don't worry! Our primary concern will be the relationships *between* the cards. As we work through the examples, you will soon become very familiar with these cards indeed.

Just like an iceberg, we see only ten percent of a tarot spread. The stunning visuals and layouts of the cards and spreads seduce the mind, which then becomes blind to what is going on underneath. Below the surface there is an intricate web of connections and interactions that can surface as insights and intuitive leaps. Sometimes we have no idea where these come from and may find ourselves unable to explain them.

A large part of the ten percent that we can see are the tarot meanings, which are often a hangover from a bygone age. Yet we still cling to them. How many times have we tried to shoehorn a recalcitrant or quaint meaning into the Ten of Swords in the future position when the client wants to know how a love affair will develop? The structure of the Tarot draped over the Tree of Life is another problem area—the nuts and bolts of sephiroth, pillars, and other technical concepts are too often meaningless when applied to the lives of our clients.

In hermeneutical terms the 'meanings' of the cards only appear when they are spread out for the client *at that moment*. Spreads like the Celtic Cross have an implicit direction of time, from the past through the present to the future. However, we are all of us a mess of contradictions once we stop to consider our notion of time. Some of us live in the future, while others live in fear of what happened in the past. How can we access all of this in the Celtic Cross?

To redress the balance, we will explore the hidden depths of the Celtic Cross spread. Catherine realised that her own interpretations of the spread were inadequate, and she supposed the technique of 'Elemental Dignities'—which she had heard of—might help, but she was unsure how to apply it to the reading. As we worked on this together, Catherine encouraged me to write in more detail about the process of uncovering the hidden ninety percent of the reading. At first, we imagined we might simply convert our emails into a narrative structure. However, the complex layers of meaning that we started to uncover forced us to re-think. Even though I have been reading the tarot for years using these techniques, I had no notion that we would find so much to explore.

Whilst we re-wrote and restructured the book, transformations occurred within both of us. Catherine's confidence at reading grew in leaps and bounds and the questions she asked became more complex, philosophical and insightful, so I was obliged to raise my own standards too. We wanted to capture this transformation as it expressed itself in our original emails, but this created its own problems. The exponential growth in our understanding created a messy and convoluted structure for the book, for this is the crucial problem with the orderly patterns of tarot spreads: they do not adequately reflect how we actually live our lives.

Our love lives and social lives, for example, are intimately bound up with our working environment—there is simply no separation. For many, home-life may be non-existent or something we try to avoid. Some of us live our lives backwards. Nothing is ever in its right place. Imbalance is everywhere.

Tarot readings should reflect the messy way that life is, otherwise how can we communicate with our clients? With 'messy' tarot spreads, perhaps? Well, we could indeed simply throw some cards onto the table and randomly pick one as the starting point, but then how could we communicate or teach the structure we personally found among the cards to another person? Some people can do this kind of reading to great effect, but is mirroring chaos really the best way forward? What if our client is actually very orderly? A reading of this type would probably not work in that case. And besides, the orderly aspects of the reader's own mind would very likely rebel against such chaos.

To overcome the problem we may resort to applying a name or title to each position in the spread, but then we become confined by the surface meanings. Some people use the imagery within the cards to help them—indeed, many well-known tarot experts suggest precisely this—but again we are dancing on the surface. How can we get to the *roots*?

We need a balance between order and chaos. We don't want titles and positions that trap us into a corner. We want the cards to reflect what is really going on, without trying to shoehorn a card into a position yet expecting it to tell us the full story. We want reliable and simple methods to get to the ninety percent of the reading that is hidden from both us and the client.

If we abandon spreads, positions and meanings, then what do we have left? Actually, a huge amount.

When we deal the cards for a Celtic Cross spread, we always put down the same number of cards in the same order. This sequence of ten cards is the only constant between readings. At the time they were written, the original instructions for the system of divination I will present in these pages emphasised that the order of the cards *should not be altered in any way*. The reason for this was that back in those days *everyone* played cards for entertainment. When people played gin or rummy, for example, they would instinctively pick up their cards and sort them by suit or number. It was this instinctive behaviour that the instruction not to alter the order was seeking to curb.

A tarot spread is, then, the sequential placement of a string of cards. The places are assigned a name or title that gives meaning to the relationship between each place and the card in that place. But from our point of view the application of names or titles becomes arbitrary. The techniques we will explore in this book depend only upon the primary sequence of the cards. The first thing we will do, then, is to restore the cards used in Catherine's Celtic Cross spread to that simple, sequential order:

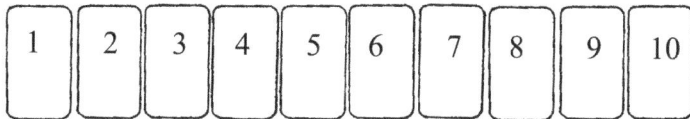

The cards are now touching each other in a line. But there are two additional methods of interpretation available to us from here. Firstly, we can look at how each card relates to its neighbours by assigning one of the four metaphysical elements (earth, water, air and fire) to each. A few simple rules allow us to do this and then arrive at a picture of the relative strengths and weaknesses of each card.

However, this elemental approach is static. Dynamism is lost. To restore it, we need a way of 'stepping through' the cards to build up a story. To achieve this we take each card in turn, using the previous elemental rules to help us, but to bring out even greater depth we assign each card a number from one to twelve, according to some simple esoteric principles that I shall describe. Then we count on from each card using this number, missing out those in-between. We can count from any card in either direction to see how it is linked to other cards through its number.

The subconscious mind works on the elemental associations, plus the counting and the linking into pairs in order to synthesise the entire process into a coherent reading. As we work on the reading some cards assume greater importance than others, and so now —everywhere we look—these same cards will keep cropping up. All the client sees, meanwhile, is us, scanning over the cards, uttering pronouncements on what is going on, most likely using very few of the words associated with the traditional divinatory meanings. This new approach can be gained from just a few logical rules and the ability to count to twelve.

This system proves particularly beneficial with respect to the court cards, which are notoriously difficult to interpret. We can now see how each court card interacts or ignores the others, just like people do in real life. One reason Catherine contacted me was her difficulty with understanding two Knights in the future positions of her Celtic Cross spread. We shall devote a lot of discussion to the subtle meanings of these cards.

Just as the ability to count is second nature, the simple laws applied to the elements also eventually become inherent in the mind. Learner drivers have difficulty coordinating the clutch, brake and accelerator pedals. Experienced drivers, on the other hand, find themselves having to think really hard if you ask them what gear they are driving in. In the same way, once the counting and elemental laws have become inherent, your mind will be left free to explore and interpret the combinations that appear.

The Structure Of The Book

In the first section of the book we shall discuss the Celtic Cross spread as it applies to the original sequence of cards in Catherine's reading. We will keep the meanings of the positions as Catherine herself learned them from the Joan Bunning Tarot Course—and you might also like to apply your own meanings to the positions, if you use them differently.

The synthesis of counting, elements, and interpretation that happens within the reader's mind is by definition impossible to replicate exactly on paper. Our first attempts at writing the book reflected this and—frankly—it soon became a mess. Structure had to be imposed, which meant separating out and describing each part of the process. When I first wrote about these techniques on my web site and in my book, *Tarot and the Magus*, I tended to discuss the elemental techniques first. Here, we shall start with Card Counting, then the Elemental Dignities, and finally Card Pairing. There are good arguments for starting with Elemental Dignities, but both systems are complete in themselves. It's your mind's ability to synthesise them that is always the key.

Card counting reveals how the cards connect to each other so that a story can be told, but we shall also add to this some extra techniques that mirror what readers often do with the Celtic Cross spread. Firstly, we shall add a significator, and then an extra card. We shall examine in depth how both cause further changes in the dynamics of the spread.

The number of permutations provided by the four elements requires some additional theory—another good reason why Card Counting is presented first. The simplest permutations concern *two* cards, and this is known as 'Card Pairing'. In the normal course of a reading, pairing is usually applied after Card Counting and Elemental Dignities. We shall extend this technique to include *three* cards, with example interpretations from both Catherine and myself. A further technique is also introduced with the inclusion of the elemental base.

There are of course times when a reading gets 'stuck'. One trick that helps with this and can create a breakthrough is to change the counting of the Aces. So we shall also examine what happens in Catherine's reading when we count eleven for the Aces.

Exploring a Tarot reading in as great a depth as this creates transformations deep within the psyche. Using the techniques described in this book, you will be in a position to offer clients readings that are out of this world. Traditionally, working with the spiritual powers associated with the Tarot has been very risky, particularly when using Western magical techniques. However, working with Card Counting and Elemental Dignities results in a natural growth in spiritual awareness. The insights that Catherine gained and which are presented here are a graphic indication of this.

The collaboration on this book between Catherine and myself was conducted entirely by email. To give a flavour of our correspondence, I have included direct quotations from Catherine's emails where appropriate.

The Celtic Cross Spread

For the most part, the Celtic Cross Spread will work for your clients, but when the problems and answers are not so clear, or when you want to add value (i.e. increase the price of your reading) then you need to know how to upgrade the reading. Since all Tarot spreads work the same way, by placing the cards in positions, we can use the techniques for reading strings of cards with *any* spread, particularly if it has between ten and twenty cards.

Often when laying out cards, readers get into a routine of placing them in the usual positions. Instead, simply pick up the first card of the spread, place it on the second card, then put those two onto the third, and so on. When you have collected all the cards in the spread, fan them out onto the table. Fanning the cards out from right to left, or left to right is a matter of personal preference, but it is important to be consistent. If you are using the Rider-Waite deck, you may need more space so that you can see which card is which. In contrast, the cards of the Thoth Tarot deck are uniquely coloured, so a large overlap is possible and they can still be distinguished easily.

Here is the original spread, as emailed to me by Catherine:

1. Heart of the Matter—Eight of Cups reversed.
2. Opposing Factor—Seven of Cups.
3. Root Cause—The Sun.
4. Past—Three of Swords reversed.
5. Attitudes & Beliefs—Four of Cups.

6. Future—Knight of Pentacles.
7. You As You Are—Ten of Wands.
8. Outside Environment—Ten of Cups.
9. Hopes & Fears—Ace of Cups.
10. Outcome—Knight of Wands reversed.

The order is there, but as we read the string of cards we will not be particularly concerned with the meanings of the positions nor, for that matter, the meanings of the cards. Throughout this book divinatory meanings have a low priority.

Some people will sometimes add extra cards into a spread to provide additional clarity. They place these cards near the card that is under question, or they will at least make the connection in their mind. Other readers may choose a Significator card and place it in proximity. These extra cards can be included in a string, as long as the order is preserved. So, if a Significator has been chosen, it can be the *first* card. If three extra cards have been added afterwards to elucidate position four ('The Past' in this case), then those cards can be added to the end of the sequence, and they will be eleventh, twelfth and thirteenth.

Seeing and understanding patterns in the cards helps us relate those patterns to the life of the client. Looking at patterns among a series of failed relationships is a good example. There may be a number of patterns that can be observed in the spread, but when there are ten cards or less these patterns may not be so obvious.

Using reversed cards is a matter of personal taste. Catherine has several reversed cards in her reading. Working with the cards in strings, reversed cards are used to indicate groups of cards, not necessarily the reversal of an individual card's meaning. Analysis using Elemental Dignities will help elucidate the relative strengths and weaknesses of the individual cards.

Pay attention to any groups of similar cards. In Catherine's reading there are two Knights, two Tens, five Cups, two Wands, one Sword and one Pentacle; one Major card, two Court cards and seven Minor cards. Three or four of a kind have greater significance than a pair.

Everyone loves a story. We use Card Counting to bring to life the story in the spread. Card Counting helps to spot and understand underlying patterns, the invisible links between the cards and their relationship to each other. It also helps us see if situations are developing for better or worse, are stagnant, or simply going around in circles. Sometimes it is possible to infer a lot about what is going on simply by looking at the card counting patterns within a reading, without interpreting the cards at all. Whatever card we start with, there will come a point when we count onto a card that has already been counted onto. This is the point when counting stops. It is usually best practice to start with the top card first in the direction of the other cards, and then in the reverse direction. Next, it is often worth counting from Court Cards that are significant in the reading. While we can count in either direction, we never change direction in mid-count. However, there is an exception: if we land on a Court card *then* we can change direction, but only if we choose to—it is not mandatory.

Clients want quick, clear answers, so if the card count meanders, or is very long, then it is often better to find a more direct route. I once remember doing a reading for a woman who had trouble finding a boyfriend. When I card counted from the top card, the count missed three male Court Cards in the string. Without even studying the cards in the sequence I was able to say that she always seemed to miss the men in her life, and she agreed.

As you count from various cards in a string you will see the patterns emerge. If you land on a card that was counted onto in a previous count, you generally do not have to go further, as you will know how the count will progress. It is amazing how the same cards show up in a count. In this case, they represent a well-trodden path, which the client is familiar with, but wants to break out from. Often what is even more significant are the cards that do not get counted onto. They are easy to miss, but with practice finding them gets easier. When you find one of these cards you need to check in both directions that none of the other cards count onto it. Uncounted cards are the source of the Nile; they represent new directions that the client has never considered, or is uncertain about taking. Generally the new direction represented by that card is worth pursuing by both reader and client. In essence, an uncounted card influences the cards either side of it, and the cards that it counts onto in either direction, but it is not influenced by these cards. You may find several uncounted cards in a string. I am sure you have had the experience of talking about something that looks so clear from the cards but means nothing to the client. It may be that this relates to an uncounted card in the spread. In Catherine's reading, the Knight of Wands is uncounted, which is how we knew he was nothing to do with her present or past circumstances. It also explained why it was so difficult for Catherine to understand anything about him. The Knight of Wands was revealed as representing a whole new life for Catherine.

Counting from each Court Card helps to see who these individuals are in the life of the client and how they interact with each other. If there are two protagonists represented by two court cards, for example, you may find that one of them counts onto the Six of Wands, 'Victory', while the other counts onto the Ten of Swords, 'Disaster'. Usually of course, things will not be so clear-cut. Using Card Counting helps us not only to avoid the clichés that too often abound with Court Cards, but also places these cards in context. When we include the divinatory meanings, we see how those meanings are changed subtly depending on the direction of the count and from or onto different cards.

Card Pairing is performed to build up extra information about the development of the reading. Start by looking at the outer cards: first and tenth, then second and ninth, and so on until you reach the centre. There will be a card at the centre if there are an odd number of cards. It is permissible to count from any card, so the pairing can start from either side. If you do not want to go through the full rigmarole of pairing, then look only at the cards in the centre of the string. Card Pairing provides an overview, and often throws up extra information that helps to link cards that were not linked in the Card Counting. (Including court cards.)

Elemental Dignities takes us away from the story provided by Card Counting, down to the details of individual cards. We use Elemental Dignities to understand how each card interacts with its neighbours within the invisible links revealed by Card Counting and Pairing. With experience, Elemental Dignities can be used at every stage of Counting and Pairing to add colour to the reading. The rules of Elemental Dignities are very simple but contain a lot of subtlety and sophistication to add nuance to the reading. Elemental Dignities can show us whether the client is blowing hot and cold over a situation, or thinks too much, or is slow to act. The Card Count for a particular card might look straightforward, but

Elemental Dignities can tell a different story if the elements alternate between Fire and Water, for example. These elements are inimical to each other and cancel each other out. We use Elemental Dignities to bring forward the subtleties of the divinatory meanings, rather than simply relying on position or whether a card is reversed.

Elemental Dignities helps us to understand the subtleties and relative strengths and weaknesses between Court Cards. Let us say we had the Queen of Disks reversed between the Knight of Wands and the Knight of Cups. We might think that because she is reversed she is weak between the two Knights, but with Elemental Dignities we know that Fire and Water weaken each other, so she is stronger than both of them.

When we combine all the techniques of Counting, Pairing and Elemental Dignities we build up a more complex picture of what is going on. We see the hidden links, we see the hidden influences, and we can tell how these will manifest and what the effect will be. We can advise our clients on which direction will be most profitable, for work, health and love and any other situation. We can see the motives of other people, hidden or otherwise, and how we can come closer to them, or avoid them altogether. As we see the pitfalls, we can advise how to avoid them, or (if that is not possible) how to minimise any problems and move toward better situations. We can also see how likely it is that the client will be able to make those changes. I mentioned that we can safely ignore the positions of the Celtic Cross when working with strings but, if you wish, you can reintroduce those positions to the interpretation (without moving the cards) and add it to all the other information you have discovered.

The Celtic Cross has a clear arrow of time from the Past to either the Future or the Outcome. But using the additional techniques you are effectively bringing in many more potential futures for your clients to choose from. Therapeutically, the more possibilities the better. Of course, as a responsible reader you will be able to advise on the best plan for action. The synergy of the Celtic Cross spread with these new techniques is greater than the sum of their parts.

With practice, the subconscious will do the work, freeing the conscious mind to interact with the client.

Now that we have an overall understanding of how these apparently disparate parts fit together, we can look at each aspect in more detail.

Paul's Analysis Of The Celtic Cross Spread

1. *Heart of the Matter — Eight of Cups reversed.*
This card is rather depressing. I always liken it to having the hangover *before* you go to the party. Hope is given up.

2. *Opposing Factor — Seven of Cups.*
Catherine does not want to be caught up in false hopes and illusion. She has been there before, and now she wants clarity, but she does not know how to get it.

3. *Root Cause — The Sun.*
Catherine is looking for success, but so far it seems to have eluded her.

4. *Past — 3 of Swords reversed.*
Clearly there has been a lot of sorrow, upset and loss. Maybe an accident or illness has contributed. Either way, we can see why it is so difficult to get beyond the Seven and Eight of Cups.

5. *Attitudes and Beliefs — Four of Cups.*
Catherine has lost her beliefs. She no longer knows what she wants, and if she did there are doubts whether the effort is worth it. She is bored with life and does not know what to do.

The Celtic Cross Spread 15

6. *Future—Knight of Pentacles.*
If we did not know already, clearly Catherine is on her own and she is looking for a partner. The good news is that he is there! He is practical, but beyond that it is difficult to say.

7. *You As You Are—Ten of Wands.*
Catherine is snowed under. She is under a lot of pressure, which could either be of her own making or from other people.

8. *Outside Environment—Ten of Cups.*
Despite the pressure represented by the Ten of Wands, it seems that there is a lot of love and happiness around, which perhaps serves to rub salt into the wounds.

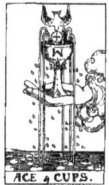
9. *Hopes and Fears—Ace of Cups.*
The Ace of Cups represents the beginning of love and happiness, but Catherine seems to be in a state of not knowing if she really wants love to come into her life, despite her comments previously.

10. *Outcome—Knight of Wands reversed*
This, I feel, is the real problem and the reason why Catherine contacted me in the first place. Her original question was: 'Will I meet the man of my dreams?'

Summary

Is her ideal outcome the Knight of Pentacles, or is it the Knight of Wands reversed? The Future is good but indeterminate, while the Outcome is of an angry and frustrated man—or is that just her perception of him? Either way, the push and pull of the two Knights is driving her crazy.

If we compare Catherine's analysis (below) with mine, it can be seen that we agree on what the reading is about. The question is how do we go beyond the surface meanings of the cards and the positions? How do we find answers to the questions and dilemmas posed in the reading?

Catherine's Analysis Of The Celtic Cross

I have been single for some time, although lingering in the background is my ex. We have both lingered and done the 'not letting go' thing. Only, I thought I had finally cracked it—my life has taken a new direction and I'm pleased to be travelling a more enlightened path. I've known for some time he's not in my future and that's okay. I think we both did something amazing for each other, which has resulted in new directions.

However, it was Valentine's Day this week and I guess I got a bit sentimental and sent him an e-card and a message. He's dating someone else now and very politely he blew me off. I had a momentary wobble, but all is well in my world again. It made me think, though, how much I would like to have someone in my life again. I've been very rigid on this point of late. Because of the work I've been doing with myself, I've held the view that I don't have the room for someone, and—to be honest—you know how it is when you fall in love; it's so time consuming (in a positive way) and your focus is shifted to this wonderful new thing in your life. So this would go against the energy and time I have given to myself. Briefly, I've read *a lot* and have tried to apply prosperity principles, enlightenment, my tarot cards—a large number of things to improve myself and develop myself as a person and spiritually. So you can see the internal conflict I have, and I think the opening three cards reflect that. The fourth card too, because it hurt, albeit briefly.

I realise now that I can have love in my life and not lose focus, if I could find someone who is travelling a similar road to my own. Then it would be a help and not a hindrance—true?

The Four of Cups is interesting because lately I have read it to mean missed opportunities, but here in this position, and to do with love, could it signal apathy and boredom? I am a commitment-phobe. So therein lies my challenge: to go for it—warts and all—commit myself and be a part of it. Most people are scared to be alone. I know it's okay to be alone, it's not scary, but I think now the opposite is true. As much as I want to be with someone, it scares me, the lifelong thing. I guess my roots are in the failed marriage and a failed relationship that I thought would last for ever. I know I have issues to deal with and ultimately I have the power to change my thinking and attitude.

I will be honest and say I do not understand the Knights. I see that they could be a person, but maybe this is the point where reading for yourself about your own love-life loses its objectivity. The Ten of Wands is correct: that is, I'm right there struggling along, balancing it all. And the Ten of Cups shows, I think, how everyone else perceives me—happy, homely and contented. The Ace of Cups is my hope and not my fear, but once again the Knight is less obvious to me.

DEALING WITH REVERSED CARDS

When there are single cards on positions in a spread, the only means of employing variation is to use reversed cards. But therein lies the problem: reversals have a binary effect; they are the *opposite* of upright cards, which tends to make the reader interpret them in a negative way. This raises issues. For example, is a 'negative' reversed card suddenly 'positive'? Having a reversed card on the 'Future' or 'Outcome' position of a spread can be devastating. This was the main reason why Catherine contacted me in the first place.

However, when we look at a string of cards, reversals have a context. We can relate the reversal to cards around it. For example, if there is a group of reversed cards we can see them as a group rather than a sequence of individually reversed cards. This becomes more significant in longer strings. If the top card of a string is reversed, it may be easier to view the other cards from this perspective, since all the other reversed cards have the same orientation to it. One benefit of this approach is that we do not have to learn an extra set of reversed meanings. However, if you are comfortable with reversed meanings, or you have learned them, then by all means incorporate them into your interpretations. As you work with the new approach you will find that it provides greater degrees of subtlety than the old either/or approach to reversals. You will discover that some aspects of a reversed card will apply and not others, and these aspects will have some influence on the surrounding cards. These subtler 'shades of grey' are more like the way in which sophisticated adults see the world.

Returning to Catherine's Celtic Cross spread, we see that the reversed cards are particularly significant. Let's look at them in more detail. Even though there are only three, they could nevertheless prove devastating.

We start with the first card, 'The Heart of the Matter': the Eight of Cups reversed. This hardly inspires confidence, does it? I can imagine the sharp intake of breath from the reader when this card was dealt out first. It refers to Catherine's current situation. The Eight of Cups is a depressing card, so if it is reversed does that mean things will improve? Catherine is not happy with her situation anyway, and if she could see an easy way out she probably would not be having the reading.

The reversed Three of Swords at the far left of the spread ('The Past') sticks out like a sore thumb. Logically, the reversed Three of Swords signifies an improvement, surely? However, Catherine knows her situation has not improved in the way she wants, so what is going on here?

The Knight of Wands reversed in the 'Outcome' position is such a let-down! Does it mean that Catherine ends with a violent man, or is he connected to the Past (Three of Swords) or the Heart of the Matter (Eight of Cups)? The only other Knight is the right way up, but he seems to be associated with her previous partner. No wonder Catherine is confused.

Looking at the Celtic Cross spread, we have the first card, the left-most card, and the last card all reversed. My sympathies are now with the poor card reader—how do you guide your client towards a more positive outlook?

Am I recommending that you do not use reversals? They are very important and I have always used them, but there are better ways of understanding them and ways of putting them in a different context.

While spreads like the Celtic Cross can highlight either 'difficult' cards, or cards that require special attention, they do not provide methods of dealing with or solving them. In later chapters I will provide some simple techniques for not only understanding why particular cards are reversed, but also for getting to grips with how they fit together into the context of the reading as a whole.

The Celtic Cross Spread

Catherine's View Of Reversed Cards

If you were to give the same spread to a hundred different tarot readers you would receive a hundred readings with differing meanings and predictions. The cards presented mean exactly what they are supposed to mean, but to *that* reader.

So how does this affect reversals? In every way. It means that the Three of Swords reversed will mean something different to me than it does to you. When I see it in a reading, I will interpret it the way *I* see it. You may see it differently, but neither way is wrong.

Much ink has been spilt on reversed meanings. Some of this I can relate to, some I can't. But none of it is wrong; the interpretations were correct at the time they were interpreted by that reader.

The problem, as I see it, with Divinatory Meanings is they usually belong to someone else. They are an expansion of an author's or reader's repertoire and may never have that same significance to anyone else.

This shows us that we have a grey area. Should we read reversals? If so, then how? Alternatively, we can choose not to read them at all. I read both ways, depending on how it suits me at the time.

When I read reversals, however, I do not see them as the opposite of the upright card. This is too narrow an approach and doesn't allow for a broader interpretation. I prefer to see the meaning of a reversed card as fading away, or not fully expressed. Perhaps there are blockages preventing the message of the card being given. Another option is that the Querent has a choice with the message of the card. If it is reversed and negative, then some work may be required by the Querent to turn the card the right way up. Conversely, if the reversal has more pleasant connotations, then the Querent must look to themselves to see what they can do to secure this more pleasant aspect.

Bearing that in mind, let's look at the three reversed cards in my original spread: the Eight of Cups, the Three of Swords and the Knight of Wands.

Upright, the Eight of Cups can mean leaving, moving on, and abandonment. This card, though, is about *choice*. The Querent has not been abandoned, but has chosen to leave. Leaving the many other layers of meaning aside, how does this translate as a reversal? To me it relates to the choice of leaving, and whether I should really do that. In the Celtic Cross reading it was in the 'Heart of the Matter' position. Splitting up and getting back together again had been a familiar theme in the relationship that appears in this reading, so this card really did sum up how I felt. As it turned out, we *weren't* getting back together, so there was some finality to it this time. There was no sadness, though; more a sense of inevitability, and in some ways relief as—on this occasion—it really was time to move on.

As Paul says, seeing the Three of Swords can really fill you with dread. In this reading, though, when I first laid out the cards and saw the Three of Swords, I had to smile. This card had been a familiar bedfellow for some time. Sitting in the position of the Past was where it belonged and, significantly, it was reversed too. For me, this reversal signified the fading of the pain associated with this relationship. It confirmed how much I had already begun to let go in order to allow healing to begin.

It was a bitter-sweet moment seeing the Knight of Wands, a male court card, in the Outcome position, but then realising he was reversed. What did it mean? I have to say I was not sure; it's what led me to contact Paul in the first place. Having one Knight in the Near Future position and one in the Outcome was a little confusing to say the least, and I worked through various scenarios of what it could mean.

These ranged from seeing two sides of the same person, to assessing that perhaps this Knight was someone who was currently unavailable to me. Maybe the blockage was my own. As I said earlier, a process of healing had begun, but was the past preventing me from finding the future? There is, of course, the traditional option of this person being undesirable, or a bad influence.

One thing is for sure—that *those* reversals were given to me in *that* reading so I could interpret them in the way that the tarot knew I would. This includes my confusion over the two Knights, because if it had been clearer to me then I would never have contacted Paul, and consequently this book would never have been written.

The Universe does indeed work in mysterious ways.

Multiple Dimensions

Tarot spreads such as the Celtic Cross work in two dimensions. Each card in the spread has a primary relationship to its position, from which we derive information. We combine the divinatory meaning with the meaning of the position to create a narrative.

This is what Catherine and I did with our interpretations of her reading. In one sense, the reading is straightforward. We can see that the reading is about problems with relationships: the Three of Swords, Ace of Cups, Ten of Cups, the Sun and the two Knights tell us this, whilst the Four, Seven and Eight of Cups show the emotional confusion that is going on. Catherine in her reading moved backwards and forwards between the cards and positions, while I worked through each position in numerical order. Catherine and I never discussed the meanings of the positions, which are of course completely open to interpretation. Fortunately, this did not cause a problem.

You could take this a step further and view the Celtic Cross spread as working in *four* dimensions—three of space and the fourth of time. The spread is a mixture of space (the situation) and time (past, present, future) according to the semantics of the names of the positions. This mixture prevails both in the positions of the cross on the left, and in the column to the right.

Positions 3, 4, 6, and 10 are primarily related to time: Root Cause, Past, Future and Outcome. It is reasonable to have the Root Cause before the Past, but how do we link them, apart from their position as third and fourth cards? What is the time-scale? It is impossible to tell. The Future card comes before the Outcome card, but there are three cards between them. 'Future' is an open-ended term, while 'Outcome' is more final and definite.

The other six cards could be seen to be either in the present moment, or to relate to space. Any of those six cards can relate to the present situation, while Space can refer to either inner or outer space. For example, 'Attitudes & Beliefs' and 'Hopes & Fears' are inner representations, while 'Outside Environment' is clearly external. 'You as You Are' could be either inner or outer, depending on the nature of the card in this position.

The first two cards, 'Heart of the Matter' and 'Opposing Factor', create a dialectic that is intended to define the nature of the whole reading. In our case we have the Eight of Cups reversed and Seven of Cups, neither of which is very specific! No wonder Catherine is confused.

Another way to understand the Celtic Cross is to see it as a snapshot of the situation. A moment frozen in time. We are asking the question of what will happen in the future based on the moment we are in, which is—of course—the moment of having a Tarot reading. Catherine's question, as no doubt are many questions of the Celtic Cross, is framed in the *future*: 'Will I meet the man of my dreams?' The cynic's answer would be: 'Not at this very moment!'

A snapshot is a snapshot—it doesn't go anywhere. For Catherine, the answer in the spread is yes, she will meet the man of her dreams, but she is worried it will be the Outcome, the Knight of Wands reversed, rather than the possibility of the Future, the Knight of Pentacles. Furthermore, the Celtic Cross does not advise her of what to do to change her situation so the 'man of her dreams' can turn up.

A snapshot is a visual metaphor. We use our sight to interpret and understand the positions of the cards in the Celtic Cross (and other spreads, also). Tarot readers draw a spatial relationship between the cards and will use the visual images of the cards themselves.

Instead, we find the specific answers to Catherine's questions within the cards and in the relationships between them. We do this without reference to their titles or the descriptions of their positions. In fact, we abandon all notion of positions relating to Past, Present, Future, Root Cause, Environment, Hopes and Fears, etc. The answers are simply in the sequence of the cards. We must realise that when we laid out the cards, we were taking them *in sequence* from the deck. We have that numeric sequence as a given; we place the cards in a line, and begin our interpretation by examining the elemental attributions of each card, seeing how they interact with one another at the elemental basis, and then we add the divinatory meanings.

To refresh, here is the original layout of the Celtic Cross spread for Catherine:

The Celtic Cross Spread   23

But here is the essential sequence and we will not be changing it:

What we will do differently, however, is to use Card Counting and Elemental Dignities.

Learning To Card Count

Card Counting is simply a system for connecting the cards and building up a story. To do so, we divide the cards into different groups.

The Minor cards from Two to Ten keep their face value. The Kings, Queens and Knights all count four. The Pages count seven. The Aces count five.

The Major Arcana is divided into three groups based mainly on astrology. The twelve Major cards associated with the zodiac signs count twelve, while the seven planetary Major cards count nine. There are three cards left over, and they count three.

THE MAJOR ARCANA	COUNT
Zodiacal: The Emperor (Aries); The Hierophant (Taurus); The Lovers (Gemini); The Chariot (Cancer); Strength (Leo); The Hermit (Virgo); Justice (Libra); Death (Scorpio); Temperance (Sagittarius); The Devil (Capricorn); The Star (Aquarius); The Moon (Pisces).	12
Planetary: The Magician (Mercury); The High Priestess (Moon); The Empress (Venus); Wheel of Fortune (Jupiter); The Tower (Mars); The Sun (Sun); The World (Saturn).	9
The Fool; The Hanged Man; Judgement.	3

The original system of Card Counting comes from the Order of the Golden Dawn, which provided a rationale behind the system. You are probably wondering why the Pages count seven, while the Major planetary cards count nine. Surely the planetary cards should count seven? In the Golden Dawn system, the Pages represent the Seven Heavens, while the planets count nine because they include the lunar nodes. Aces count five because they are the Quintessence or fifth element ('Akasha' or 'Space') from which the four elements emanate.

For the purposes of this book we will not delve deeper into these mysteries, but you can find out more from my previous book, *Tarot and the Magus*.

Card Counting starts from one, which is the first card itself. In our example this is the Eight of Cups. It itself is 'one'. We can then count 'two' in either direction, and we keep on counting until we land on a card that has already been counted onto. Once we have counted from the first card, we can then count from other cards which are significant to the reader or the client, depending on how the reading is going. So, for example, if when we count from the first card, the count does not hit a court card that represents the love interest, it is often important to find out which cards *do* count onto the court card.

We are going to count through Catherine's cards using all the techniques described so far, including some extra ones where appropriate, so we can see how the dynamics of the reading change. In this way we shall demonstrate the range and subtlety gained from reading the cards using this technique.

There are many levels of meaning and interpretation, but for starters we will keep things simple. Card counting can begin from any card in the string and we can count in either direction from each card. In practice it is best to start with either card at the end of the string. In this case we shall examine the Eight of Cups. The initial card count gives us a feeling for what is happening, and from it we start to see patterns emerge.

In a normal reading the reader will be counting through the cards, giving a running interpretation, and the Querent may make comments or interjections, which often in themselves give clues as to which of the card counts will be most profitable, or will indicate which cards in the sequence are the most important. Very often I will silently card count from several cards to get a feel of what is happening before I say anything. Sometimes I point to each card with my finger, sometimes I mentally card count.

We know that Catherine's interest lies in the two Knights, so once the card counts for the Eight of Cups have been completed we will explore these two men. Ordinarily, Court cards are considered difficult to interpret but, as you will see, with card counting it is easy to understand how they fit into a reading.

Catherine and I wrote the card counting sequences separately and the commentaries have been subsequently combined so we can compare the thought processes and interpretations. Catherine has the advantage of knowing her life, so she is able to interpret the cards in the light of this experience whilst I, as the reader, do not know the details, so my analysis is generally shorter. If this had been a normal reading Catherine would have been interpreting my words and applying them to her situation.

As you work through the card counting you will notice that the same cards are part of the count, but note also how the interpretations of them differ.

COUNTING RIGHT FROM THE EIGHT OF CUPS

Catherine

Starting with the Eight of Cups and counting to the right, we hit the Ten of Cups, which is supported by the Ace of Cups, signifying the bringing of new love to an already established, happy home or family. The Ten of Wands could be reminding us of the responsibility we have in balancing this situation, the extra burden of someone else in the family line-up. Being a single parent, I see myself very much as the Ten of Wands, solely carrying the burdens and obligations of my family. I wonder if there is any room for another in my life and it looks as if I'm saying: 'I want this new love, it's knocking on my door, but I have all this other stuff I have to do and I do not know if I have the time or the energy to let it in.'

Paul

We start with a feeling of lethargy and indolence.

Ten of Cups

Paul

This card relates to happiness and the family, so we know there is something not right with the home. The next card gives us a clue.

Ten of Wands

Catherine

From the Ten of Cups we go to the Ten of Wands, which is flanked by the Ten of Cups and the Knight of Pentacles. Could we be looking at the new love as the Knight, answering the concerns of the Ten of Wands? Perhaps a balance can be achieved with this Knight's influence.

Paul

Oppression. Catherine feels something weighing down on her. The next card will tell us where that oppressive feeling is coming from.

Knight of Pentacles

Catherine

From the Ten of Wands we go to the Knight of Pentacles, who now falls under the spotlight! The Ten of Wands is nagging him with its burden and on the other side we have the Four of Cups. The Knight remains the strongest, although this is a passive situation. He doesn't look to be receiving any help from either side when we consider the apathy and inaction of the Four of Cups and the weight of the Ten of Wands. He is in the principal position and he is the strongest elementally—we could say he is going it alone. Could he really be the Knight in shining armour? Could I be looking at someone who can help with those burdens but can keep the passion and interest alive? I have been involved with a Court Pentacle before and the Four of Cups is potentially a worry. It's good this has been highlighted, because it is a side of me that I need to deal with. I fear I have commitment issues and this card could be showing me a potential downside to a relationship with this Knight, or my need to embrace a future relationship fully.

Paul

A man! Catherine does not have a man in her life, so it is either her ex-partner, or she is thinking about a man in the future. Is it romantic?

Ace of Cups
Catherine

Next in line is the Ace of Cups. Would it be feasible to say the Knight of Pentacles is the new love? Apart from stabilising the family home he has taken us straight to the Ace—the symbol of new love. This Ace is in a strong position, despite the Fire on one side from a reversed Knight of Wands. It is strengthened by the Ten of Cups on the other side. It's funny how the joyous family scene of the Ten is now supporting the idea of new love, as opposed to the Ace trying to nudge its way in. It seems when we looked at the Knight as a potential love interest, we had some reservations, but when he looks back at us, we see all the possibilities, not even the negative Knight can really dampen this scene.

Paul

There is definitely a sense here of the new love that she wants.

The Sun
Catherine

After hitting the Ace we head to the Sun, the card we need for happiness. However, it doesn't look very encouraging. Looking at these three cards, the Sun is what we would hope for: love, warmth, vitality. But it is directly flanked by the Seven of Cups, representing fantasy, illusion and imagination. What does this mean? That this is my fantasy and nothing more? The pain represented by the Three of Swords reversed could mean it is a futile exercise that will only lead to pain and heartache. Since the Seven and Three are friendly to each other, then is it a question of choice? There are two Knights here, after all. Will choosing the wrong one end in tears?

Paul

She is looking for success in love, a man that she can respect, and help with her family.

Eight of Cups and Summary
Catherine

So we have gone full circle. We began from a position of despondency and despite a journey through some light, we ended here again. This suggests repeated mistakes and incorrect decisions.

Why is that? What on earth has happened? Looking at this clinically, I think I know the answer: it lies with the Knight and my perception.

Looking at this sequence, we went straight to the happy home of the Ten of Cups, which pointed out the weight of responsibility that arises from that scene. From there we went to the Knight, the most stable of them all. Herein lies the problem. Am I looking for a Knight in shining armour to rescue me from the weight of the Ten of Wands? Is my longing for love for the wrong reasons? If I wanted to be rescued then no wonder this path is trouble! The beginning of the new love looked apparently bright, but it was blighted and cannot sustain either of us under these circumstances, so we ended up back in despair.

Paul

When we start from the Eight of Cups, we end the count on the Eight of Cups in one direction, and the Seven Cups in the other direction. These cards are next to one another, and so we can reasonably assume that they refer to the past. Perhaps Catherine is having trouble leaving her past behind.

The two cards common to both directions are the Knight of Pentacles and the Sun. It is fascinating to see the strong connection between these two.

If we compare the two counts we find that they include every card except one—the Knight of Wands, who appears as the Outcome card in the Celtic Cross spread! Already, then, we see that the Knight of Wands (potentially her new man) might well have nothing to do with her present situation, which I think is very good.

In one direction we count from the Eight of Cups onto itself, and in the other direction we arrive on the Seven of Cups, next to it. When the cards are circular, we know that in real life things are going around in circles and since the Knight of Wands is outside those circles, we would have to advise Catherine to look elsewhere.

We would never have found this pattern in a standard Celtic Cross spread.

Counting Left From The Eight Of Cups

Three of Swords

Catherine

Beginning from the Eight of Cups and counting to the left, we land on the Three of Swords. It is fair to say I have felt the pain of the Three of Swords recently. The reason I wanted this reading is because of a significant break-up. So, although this card looks scary, I can relate it to my past. That's where it was represented in the Celtic Cross Spread, and I hope this is not influencing me, but there is no denying the relevance of the Three to my past. Paul said earlier that the Sun represents my sentimental attachment to the past and that I may be trying to recreate it. In this sequence, the Sun could also be trying to shine light on past mistakes, so that they aren't repeated. I find the Four of Cups a little harder to place here, though thinking back to my commitment issues, this could be showing how my fear of commitment is related to the pain of the Three, so I keep myself guarded and unresponsive to new situations because of where it may lead—in this case, a return to pain.

Paul

She is really feeling alone.

Seven of Cups

Catherine

Next in line is the Seven of Cups, which to be honest has always been a bit of a mysterious card to me. It has the Sun to its right and it is supported on its left by the Eight of Cups reversed. These do not seem the best of cards. The Eight of Cups signifies leaving, withdrawal, which is true of the broken relationship related to the Three of Swords. Its reversal is interesting, particularly if we look at it with the Seven of Cups. If there were other choices, if there was the possibility that this relationship could work, then we would not be walking away, we would be staying put. How many of these choices, though, are real? Considering the length of time it took for this relationship to accept its end, what was it based on? How many decisions were based on illusions; not half-truths, but fantasies, *wanting* to believe? The weakness of the Sun is also relevant; it may be trying to shine a light, or trying to be its own light, but under all these illusions, it falters.

Paul

She does not how to express her feelings on the subject.

Knight of Pentacles

Catherine

We follow the Seven of Cups to the Knight—where we have been before, but this time we have come from a different direction. In the first string we dealt with the home and family and were led to the Knight from there. We have come to him now from dealing directly with painful feelings and facing the past. He could be the one to help heal the pain of the past and show that I can let down my guard and be open to this Knight in shining armour and all that he can bring. With the Ten of Wands to his right, it looks now as if he has control over those burdens and doesn't seem troubled by either.

Paul

It may be that she is unable to express her feelings about him and perhaps this relates to the past.

The Sun

Catherine

After hitting the Knight we change direction and head to the Sun, the sign we need for a happy ending. But again, as above, it is flanked by the Seven of Cups, representing fantasy. So again I'm left wondering whether this is just my fantasy, or that a wrong choice might lead to the heartache of the Three of Swords.

Paul

Again, this might be the past happiness she is trying to re-create.

Four of Cups

Catherine

Counting from the Sun, we next go to the Four of Cups, which could be seen as being held down by the Three, pain being the result of any action. The Knight reinforces the Four by giving it backbone and belief—which is in direct conflict with the Three.

Paul

There is a kind of numbness associated with this card. She has gone through feelings and now she has nothing to feel—is this all there is?

Seven of Cups

Catherine

From the Four of Cups we end up back with the Seven of Cups, and so ends the count with this path.

Paul

This completes the loop. Catherine really does not know how to feel, or how to move on. Perhaps this is the key?

Summary

Catherine

It looks as though I am still looking for the Knight to fix all my problems. From the sad and despondent beginning we land straight on the painful Three of Swords, a stark reminder of that break-up, straight into the arms of the Knight. And despite my pride in not doing that, it seems time is irrelevant and that maybe after all my talk of being over this and in control, am I really? Do I see this Knight as a saviour? It doesn't look well because heading to the Sun (as we have found out) is misleading, for despite its strength in a regular tarot reading, here, elementally, it's in a supporting role and even under attack. Finding out all is not well would leave anyone despondent and apathetic, and this is what I am looking at with the Four of Cups. The honeymoon is surely over and all is definitely not well.

Paul

We seem to be looking backwards in this string of cards. Catherine is looking back at the pain and loss of the past. She is having trouble understanding her own emotions. Does she want him back in her life?

Counting Right From The Knight Of Pentacles

Knight of Pentacles

Catherine

Since we have identified the Knight of Pentacles as a possible person in my future, it seems only fitting to see where he would take us if we conducted a count from him. The following sequence then is a possible path that could be encountered if I joined with this Knight.

Paul

The Knight is almost at the centre of the sequence of cards, perhaps representing how Catherine has seen him in her life.

Ace of Cups

Catherine

We go straight from the Knight of Pentacles to the Ace of Cups. We couldn't ask for a better start. But there are questions. Does it mean that although drawn in by the premise of new love, he has settled very easily and quickly into the family? We also have the Knight of Wands making an appearance on the right of the Ace, perhaps knocking on the door of love too? The Ace of Cups seems to offer much, but it seems like a double-edged sword. On one side we have that happy homely scene, but on the other, perhaps all is not what it seems. Is the Knight of Wands already on the scene throwing a spanner in the works?

Paul

We go straight to the Ace of Cups—a gift of love? Maybe, but we already know he represents her past. Is she looking for someone similar?

The Sun

Catherine

If we follow the count of five we land with the Sun, and as we have said before, on the surface it looks good to land here from the Ace of Cups. But all is not as it seems and I cannot help but see a storm here now. The heat from the Sun heats up the ocean surface and results in convection, which can produce a maelstrom. It makes me wonder why we have such an unstable situation. Is this something to do with the Knight of Wands? We do have some menacing clouds on the Three of Swords but, as some would say, the Sun is breaking through those clouds, so maybe this situation is in the past or fading from significance? Perhaps this is the fallout and the aftermath in one triplet? Is the Sun not only the life-giving force but the healer too, calming and settling that aftermath?

Paul

Catherine expects him to be strong and successful.

Eight of Cups
Catherine

From the Sun we land on the Eight of Cups. It doesn't look good does it? That volatile situation with the Sun has taken its toll and I am now facing the possibility of walking away again. It's interesting that between the Sun and the Eight of Cups is the Seven of Cups, the card of choices, fantasy, disillusionment and excesses. How much of an effect is it having on me? Am I being shown here that my choices are many, that I am in the driving seat and it's all down to me? Too many choices and I switch off. I can see why I am walking away here.

Paul

Did he cause her depression in the first place? Or are we seeing his depression?

Ten of Cups
Catherine

And home to a happy scene. But do I have the Knight with me? Or did I leave him behind? It's difficult to say, but I have gone home nonetheless. On closer inspection though, the strongest card is the Ace of Cups. It seems I did leave the Knight behind as I am still looking for love. I have completed a cycle without hitting another card. There is a pattern here and I can see it now, and it's about to be repeated.

Paul

He stayed with her because of the children.

Ten of Wands

Catherine

Although we have not seen the Ten of Wands in this path, we have seen it in this spread, often coupled with the Ten of Cups. It is the pressure and the balancing act required to sustain that happy home. The Knight is in this triplet too, and although he is a moderator, he is the strongest card. He can see the pressure I am under, he is looking straight at me with all those wands on my back and he wants to help.

Paul

Bringing up children on your own is not easy, and here we see the pressure was too much.

Knight of Pentacles

Catherine

From the Ten of Wands we end up back on the Knight of Pentacles and so ends the count for this path.

Paul

It appears that he is also going around in circles.

Summary

Catherine

I was looking forward to seeing what would happen in this count, and although it was not a future I would want to engage in, it has shown me repeated mistakes I have made and—without awareness—could make again. Getting into a relationship for the wrong reasons can have dire consequences, and I can see it in this path.

Paul

This sequence of cards enforces the perception that we are looking at the past, of how she thought she had loved, but things went wrong and she found herself under pressure. Since we are looking at the Knight, perhaps he represents Oppression to her in some way.

Counting Left From The Knight Of Pentacles

Catherine chose to summarise this card count, which is not surprising when we consider my analysis.

Knight of Pentacles

Did his family have high expectations, or does he have a large ego?

The Sun

The Sun next suggests that he did.

Four of Cups

He also seems to have been bored or lost interest.

Seven of Cups

His emotions were confused. The Seven of Cups often represents drink or drug problems.

Knight of Pentacles

He is going around in circles.

Summary

Catherine

I am cutting straight to the summary because I am getting the message this time and it doesn't need saying again. Beginning from the Knight of Pentacles, this time we are looking left and going straight to the Sun and the maelstrom. If I did not get the message loud and clear before, this time it's being shouted from the rooftops! Apathy soon sets in and we feel disillusioned. No matter what the Sun can do, this is a repeated cycle that I do not want to get back into.

The only difference here is ending back on the Knight of Pentacles, and to be honest, he is getting on my nerves now. He is just not going away, he is at every turn and—so far—in every path I have looked at.

Paul

The lack of ambition or energy to do anything about his situation is striking.

Counting Right From The Knight Of Wands

Knight of Wands

Catherine

This sequence begins with the very quiet Knight of Wands. He has been there on the sidelines all the way through this exercise, not doing much or saying much. It would be fair to say he may have played a bigger role if we had ended some of the other sequences with the Ace of Cups and not another card. But our guidelines stipulate a count of five, using the eleven only if necessary—in which case the Ace of Cups only lands repeatedly on itself. It could signify the leaving of both of these Knights for pastures new, but that would be the last thing I would want. That would be like speed-dating. No thanks!

Paul

The Knight is the key to the reading because so far he has not shown up in any card count. He is new energy.

The Sun
Catherine

And so to the Sun. And back to the maelstrom. I do not like this repeating the way it is. I can see how the Sun may well be trying to shed light on the pain of the Three of Swords next to it: the sun breaking through those storm clouds. After all, fire is no enemy of air. True it is weakened by the water, but it is the planetary Sun, and it doesn't get any hotter than that! The triplet it belongs to still grabs me, even after all this analysis. I've amazed myself by how many variations I have seen with it. That said, this is still a hotbed of a triplet. Maybe it's not such a problem for a Knight whose element is fire; perhaps he is at home here, untroubled by the activity, being active and adventurous, and this may even be attractive to him. He may be a proactive type of guy and choose easily, untroubled by the excesses in front of him.

Paul

The Sun next suggests that this is so.

Eight of Cups
Catherine

From the Sun to the Eight of Cups. And what do we make of this? Is he perturbed by the triplet of the Sun enough to leave? Is he leaving, or is it me again? Was the encounter with the Sun a rocky start to a relationship that could go further? There are many questions here, I hope they will be answered below.

Ten of Cups
Catherine

And so back home again, to the warmth and sanctity. But the home is not the strongest card in this triplet, the Ace of Cups is. How interesting that we are seen to be leaving in the Eight of Cups and, while I think I am heading home, I am really heading back to my desire again. Unless I deal with the issues I have then all I will end up doing is repeating the mistakes of the past and treat new love unfairly, creating new cycles that I will eventually have to break. No time like the present, then.

Ten of Wands
Catherine

And back to the pressure and the responsibility and the burden. I have to say though, despite the weight of this card, the wands do not fall, so although I may have felt like I need rescuing by a Knight in shining armour, I am actually coping quite well all by myself. I thought I had myself pretty much pegged before this reading, but I have learned so much about myself, this has been a great lesson in more ways than one.

Knight of Pentacles
Catherine

Enter, stage left! And here he is, right on time, regular as clock work, the most reliable Knight in the deck. He is still looking at me struggling, but this time I am not asking for help. This is intriguing, to stumble upon this Knight during this path. Is there a love triangle? Or a choice of suitors? What is different now is that even if the Knight of Wands has maybe left the stage, I am not seeing this Knight through my Disney eyes, though in a minute I may well feel I'm in the middle of joust.

Ace of Cups
Catherine

Arriving at the Ace of Cups and I am somewhat intrigued by the influence the Knight of Wands is having in this sequence. He has been silent throughout, but he is coming into his own now. He is the weakest element in this triplet, totally overrun by the water, but while I am looking at this Ace now, I see him like I have not seen him before and I don't know why. I have managed to hide in the safety and sanctity of my home life when I felt I needed to, but it seems that either side of the Ace is a choice, the safety of the home or the adventure of the Knight.

Summary
Catherine

When I first glanced at this sequence, I thought it would be the one I would want to work for; the analysis, however, has shown that it would not be trouble-free.

The Knight of Wands trod a similar path to the Knight of Pentacles—and, funnily enough, the Eight of Cups—when they all went to the right. What is different about them are their natures. I think the Knight of Wands handles the powerful triplet of the Sun better because he is a fire element. Whatever causes the troubles at the beginning of either of these relationships, causing one of us to leave, it's still present, and so it must be with me. Since the air is the strongest in that triplet, then I think the blockage is with the pain of my past—the Three of Swords. I need to address that, even release it. I also need to learn to stop running.

Paul

I have seen this kind of pattern many times in a reading. As soon as we start to move on from previous patterns, we are confronted with those patterns, and we are challenged to see if we have learned from them. That is when the fears arise again.

COUNTING LEFT FROM THE KNIGHT OF WANDS

Ten of Wands
Catherine

Taking the count to the left, the direction the reversed Knight is facing and we land on the Ten of Wands. We have not hit the Ten of Wands like this before, as the first hit in a sequence. My first thoughts are 'oh, great, more difficulty'. But is the man carrying the Ten of Wands on his back now the Knight of Wands? If he is, then he is giving the Knight of Pentacles a run for his money. This is the first time the burden has been taken from me without asking. This seems to have potential.

Paul

Catherine does not expect an easy time with any man in her life. Maybe she expects that either he gives her a hard time, or she gives him a hard time.

Ten of Cups
Catherine

If the Knight of Wands is really carrying all those wands on his back, and carrying the burden, then by landing on the happy Ten of Cups he is coming home, to our home. True to form, instead of being excited I feel apprehensive; better not get my hopes up. I do have an internal mountain to climb.

Paul

This card is good for happiness, but it does not necessarily last.

Ace of Cups
Catherine

This has not happened before, the Ace being in this position. The new love represented here appears after the Knight of Wands has taken a share of the burden and seemingly slotted into the sanctity of the family. I am not keen to introduce anyone into my home so easily, so I can only presume that this Knight comes to me as a friend first, and then as my lover or partner. It would make sense of the order presented here, one that has broken with the cycles repeated so far.

Paul

Certainly, Catherine wants to see if he can work with her children before there can be love.

Four of Cups
Catherine

Well, who said it would last! If I have learned nothing else about myself, it is that I am cynical. That said, I do have this card and its meaning to deal with. It's the strongest in its triplet and although I do not care for its message, I have seen it enough to know that I have to learn to deal with quiet times. If life was high all the time, we would all be exhausted and seek out the peace and quiet anyway.

Paul

She sees the love degrade into a familiar pattern. Things go off the boil.

Seven of Cups

Catherine

Oh, more choices! Or more imaginings from a bored old me? I've been intrigued by these two cards, their apparent connections and possible meanings. It doesn't seem to be an accident that there are so many cups on offer in two separate cards. What is the difference between them? Their reality or their potential? The Seven of Cups can mean disillusionment and I have said that in this analysis, but it can also mean the imagination, which can be made real. I am skirting the issue, but what I'm really suggesting is do I draw the Knight of Pentacles back to me out of sheer boredom or apathy? I hope not, but he is the next card in the sequence.

Paul

How disillusioned will she become?

Knight of Pentacles

Catherine

So he does come back on the scene, and did he ever really leave? The only thing we can see for sure is he is in the sequence and being counted just like the rest. What I would really want to know is if he is back on his own accord, or have I had a direct effect on his appearance. And the question has to be asked—is he present *physically*, or is the familiarity of this sequence of cards reminding me of how things were with him and so I try to avoid his influence?

Paul

She expects the Knight of Wands to revert to type, the sort of man she has had in her past—the Knight of Pentacles.

The Sun

Catherine

Back to this hot, arid situation. Looking at how we got here, are we in for a bit of a testing time? Is the maelstrom right here in my life? And who really is at the centre of it? I am hoping it is the two Knights because I want to appear to be an upstanding moral person, but I do not know at this point. What I do know is I am looking at the Seven of Cups again, albeit in a secondary role. Will it dampen down the Sun or will the Sun extinguish it? One thing is for sure, the air is doing just fine and, being the Three of swords, we might say it could be better, but we cannot dress up what is there, we have to deal with it. We arrived at the Sun from the Knight of Pentacles in the path of the Knight of Wands—it could look better than this, I think! I also wonder how much the Knight of Pentacles is offering to bring light back to my life. I think that would be futile, though, as the other paths have shown me what loops I end up in with him.

From the Sun we land up ironically back at the Four of Cups. Bored. Did I lose them both?

Paul

Hope springs eternal.

Four of Cups

Catherine

Back to boredom again.

Summary

Catherine

That was quite a journey. It started well and did not end perhaps the way I would have liked, but hey, this is the real world, not Mills & Boon. What I think I need to add to the triplet of the Sun is *hope*. The Three of Swords is reversed, and although I do not care for 180 degree reversals, I do accept reversals as blockages, or that the card is not fully expressed. I feel I need some hope at the end of this spread and thinking back to the light breaking through the clouds in this card, and the fact that it is next to the strongest fire card, the Sun, then I can only hope that all is not lost and that whatever damage may occur, there is hope after all.

Paul

For many Tarot readers, the presence of the Three of Swords is problematic. However, here the Three of Swords shows that Catherine needs to make a break, to move on, before she can grow and find new love, otherwise she will be going from the frying pan into the fire.

Understanding The Four Elements

The best way to understand the four elements is through the four suits of the Minor Arcana, in which the entire range of an element is represented.

Since the Aces include all the qualities of their element, we will represent the elements as the Aces.

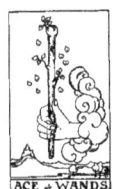

Fire — Action
The Wands or Fire cards represent actions, deeds and consequences of actions. Fire is hot, aggressive, dynamic and unstable.

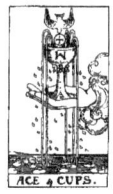

Water — Emotions, Desires
The Cups or Water cards represent emotions and feelings. Water is cold and passive.

Air — Thoughts, Problems
The Swords or Air cards represent thoughts and ideas. Air is hot, wet, divisive and unstable.

Earth — Practicality
The Disks or Pentacles or Earth cards represent practicality, business and money. Earth is solid, dry and cold.

There are many more attributions that can be applied, but I want to keep things simple for now. As we progress, we will see that from simple building blocks we can build more complex structures. To understand the development of the elements, we will firstly consider paired cards of the same element and then three cards of the element. After this we will consider pairs and triplets containing more than one element.

CARDS OF THE SAME ELEMENT

Reading cards in isolation is not always very helpful, so an alternative is to consider paired cards of the same element.

Two Fire cards represent actions that bounce off each other but have nowhere to go. It's like when two people politely say: 'You go,' 'No, you go.' At some point one of the cards has to stop acting so the other can proceed. If not, paradoxically, nothing can happen.

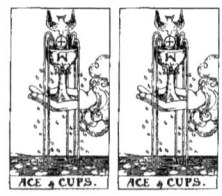

Two Water cards increase the level of passivity. Because neither have anything to push against, the desire is to merge and there is no other energy except their own inertia. The desire to unite is strong, but there will equally be a level of frustration.

Understanding The Four Elements 47

 Two Air cards are like two people arguing, but because they are not prepared to change their views the debate becomes sterile.

 Two Earth cards sit there, unmoving, not communicating, almost oblivious to each other.

Three Cards With The Same Element

As we can see, paired cards of the same element have nowhere to go—they need a third card for progress to occur. In the examples below, the centre card is the extra card. The energies of the outer cards will tend to concentrate on the centre card.

 The two outer Fire cards rush to the centre card, but because it is also Fire there is nothing to contain it. As a result the energy will spew out onto whatever is next. It is like a chain reaction that is unstoppable.

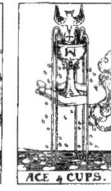 The two outer Water cards can now merge with the centre card; they lose themselves in it.

The two outer Air cards can now engage in a proper discourse, so they can move from their intellectual positions into a new view.

Now the two outer Earth cards have the potential to work together, but they each retain their own identity, providing support to the centre card.

THREE CARDS IN THE OTHER DIRECTION

We analysed three cards going from the outer to the inner, but the direction can go the other way, from the centre card to the outer cards. In the previous examples, the energy was concentrated, but in the opposite direction the energy is more likely to be dispersed.

Three Fire Cards

The energies of the centre card are divided between the outer cards. We can also see this as an expansion of the energy, which can increase or decrease depending on the nature of the cards. The outer cards are a dual expression of the energy of the centre card.

Three Water Cards

Water flows outward or is diluted from the centre card to the outer cards. We can view this as leakage or seepage because there is nothing to contain the flow. This might represent someone who is emotionally being pulled in two directions.

Three Air Cards

The intellectual focus of the centre card becomes confused as the two opposing ideas pull it apart. This is the state of being unable to make a choice.

Three Earth Cards

The centre card will resist the inertia of the outer cards, so all retain their identity. There is no movement or change, but there is a consolidation of the energy. This represents the building of a strong foundation.

CIRCULAR ENERGY

We have seen how energy can flow from the centre card to the outer cards, and conversely from the outer cards to the centre card. But there is another way in which the energy may flow: in a circle between the cards. We can visualise this better if we imagine the cards as the sides or points of an equilateral triangle, in which case any of the cards can be regarded as being at the 'centre'.

Three Fire Cards

The energy flows continuously; it may condense or it may expand. Where the energy enters and exits will depend on the nature of the cards.

Three Water Cards

The Waters tend to merge; the overall quality will depend on the mix of cards. For example the Three of Cups, Nine of Cups and Ten of Cups will point to greater joy, while the Five, Seven and Eight of Cups will tend to depress.

Three Air Cards

This will result in the spouting or unfolding of intellectual knowledge and creativity—like a kind of 'brainstorming'. Too many ideas will result in confusion.

Three Earth Cards

This suggests resistance to the flow of energy and a lack of interchange. Identity is maintained, leading to solidity and strength but also immovability.

For the most part, your interpretations will be from the centre card to the outer cards, but it's useful to keep in mind the other possibilities.

Changing The Dynamics

Traditionally, the first thing a tarot reader does at the start of the tarot reading is to pick a Significator, which is removed from the tarot deck and placed on the table. The rest of the cards are then shuffled and dealt. The Significator is usually a Court card that resembles the client.

Catherine didn't choose a Significator for her reading, but—as it turned out—there were two of them in the spread, the two Knights. Using the methods of Card Counting we have been able to say a lot about these two men, far more than would be possible with the standard Celtic Cross layout.

As we have seen, we never change the sequence of the cards—it remains sacrosanct. But if we had chosen a Significator, where would it have gone in the string? Because it is the first card to be chosen, the obvious place for it would be at the beginning or at the left end of the string. So how does this change the Card Counting?

Remember that although we fan out the cards in a line, they are counted as if they are in a circle. In this case it doesn't matter if we place the Significator at the beginning or end of the string, it will still be between the same cards. Try it out for yourself. In Catherine's spread it would be between the Eight of Cups reversed and the Knight of Wands reversed. However, it's reasonable simply to place the Significator on the left side of the string.

Several groups of cards will be affected:

1. Most of all, the Eight of Cups reversed and the Knight of Wands reversed, and the cards either side of them.
2. The cards and their neighbours that are counted onto by the Significator.
3. And the Significator itself will be modified by the cards that count onto it.

Unless you are reading for a teenager, the Significator will generally be either a Knight, Queen or King, and the card count will always be four. If you are using Catherine's version of the Celtic Cross, then the Root Cause and the Outside Environment positions will be directly connected.

Catherine is a mother, so we will choose the Queen of Pentacles as her Significator. The full reasons for this choice are explained below, but for now we will place the Significator at the beginning of the sequence of cards. As mentioned, in our example it is in effect between the Eight of Cups reversed and Knight of Wands reversed.

THE EFFECT ON ELEMENTAL DIGNITIES AND CARD COUNTING

The element of the Significator will directly influence the cards closest to it—the Eight of Cups and the Knight of Wands, and the cards that *they* are closest to.

If we choose the Significator before we deal the cards we will have no control over this, but if we pick the Significator afterwards (as we did in this case), we can be clever. Catherine is an adult with children, so our Significator will be a Queen, but which element to choose? Normally we would choose the Significator by personality, but this system allows us to be more sophisticated.

Before we include the Significator, we know that Cups (Water) and Wands (Fire) are inimical, so choosing the Queen of Cups or the Queen of Wands for the position in the string that the Significator is about to occupy is not a good idea. This leaves us with the

Queen of Swords or the Queen of Pentacles, both of which are friendly with Fire and Water. Also, we know that Air and Earth are under-represented in the entire string of cards. Having Air or Earth as a Significator will strengthen the elemental balance of the reading. Air cards generally represent problems, while Earth cards suggest practicality and grounding, so we will select the Queen of Pentacles and immediately the first and last cards are strengthened.

Unless we choose a Page, which counts seven, we know that the Significator will directly count four onto the third card from the left, and the third card from the right. In our example these will be the Sun and the Ten of Cups respectively. This is the most obvious change, but the addition of the Significator will cause a ripple effect throughout the card counting. Except for card counts that do not pass over the Significator (which would be very short ones) every other card count will change in some way.

So far, we have seen how the Knight of Pentacles is strongly involved in the card count, while the Knight of Wands is entirely disconnected. Will the addition of the Queen of Pentacles make a difference?

COUNTING FROM THE QUEEN OF PENTACLES

In one direction the count is very simple. Counting four from the Queen we hit the Sun, and from there we count nine—and we are back to the Queen. I think this represents a very simple idea, that of Catherine wanting happiness and success in her life, but she has to know that it must come from within. Circular card counts such as this one are generally not productive—after all, we have not really gone anywhere.

In the opposite direction there is more movement—and a surprise. Counting four we land on the Ten of Cups, which is under pressure from the Ten of Wands, but supported by the nascent Ace of Cups. Counting ten we then hit the Knight of Wands! At last, a card that connects to this elusive man. Counting four takes us to the Ten of Wands, Oppression, so even though we are connecting with the Knight the picture is hardly cheerful, but let's move on. Next, we land on the Ace of Cups, so even though there is a lot of pressure, there is nonetheless a sense that the relationship can work. Counting five takes us to the Four of Cups, and then the Seven of Cups, which are hardly inspiring, particularly when the final count lands on the Ten of Wands. I would say that even though the Knight is part of the count, Catherine does not exactly expect miracles.

The Sun is the only card that connects to the Queen, so in a sense she is still isolated. Since the Sun is highlighted, it is worth checking what other cards connect to the Sun, and the surprise is that there is only one other card—the Knight of Pentacles! Look closely at the string of cards and you will see that the Sun is equidistant from the Queen of Pentacles and the Knight of Pentacles. In other circumstances, I guess you would see this as a good sign, but we know that the Knight of Wands is where Catherine wants to be.

Card counting has this uncanny knack of selecting cards that are pertinent—it sorts out the wheat from the chaff. Now we know that the addition of the Queen connects to the Knight of Wands, we want to know if there are other ways he can be brought into the equation. To do that, we need to know what cards connect to and from the Knight, and again we have a very short, exclusive list. I have already mentioned the Ten of Cups—and that is it. We are making progress. The Ten of Cups is a positive card for relationships, and it is part of the count from the Queen, so it seems that she has to make the effort to go toward him, wherever he is.

Catherine's Summary Of The Queen Of Pentacles

The Queen of Pentacles is strongest and comfortable. Though we are lacking thought or rationality, we do have action and emotion which are grounded.

I had thought I was the Eight of Cups, doing the walking. Now that my Significator, the Queen of Pentacles has been added to the layout, I can see my involvement. I realise now that I was a spectator, viewing from a safe point. By adding the Queen to the cards I am becoming an active player. It seems ludicrous to say that, because this is of course *my* life, but I just had not viewed it that way. I now see the Eight of Cups as action and not as myself.

Including Temperance

Catherine decided to draw an extra card to elucidate the reading. It was the Temperance card. The question was, where to place it? We can put it at either end of the string, but it would be better to place it at the right-hand side, next to the Knight of Wands. Whichever end we put it, it will be between the Eight of Cups and the Knight of Wands.

Because Temperance is related to Sagittarius it is a Fire card, which will strengthen the isolated Knight of Wands. We have not had a combination of two Fire cards with a Water card before, so we can see that the Eight of Cups is now very weak.

The Ace of Cups is adjacent to the Knight of Wands, and this card will also be weakened by the two Fire cards. (You may have noticed by now that not much weight is awarded to reversed cards in this system, and we are making no exception here for the reversed Knight of Wands.)

Since Temperance is a zodiac sign we count twelve, which has an interesting effect. When we card count from Temperance we find it counts onto itself! This card has 'short-circuited' itself. We get the same result in both directions. There is a simple rule at work: if the number of cards in the string is one less than the card being counted it will count onto itself. If there had been nine cards in the string a Ten would have counted onto itself.

The next stage is to see which cards count onto Temperance. I suggest that for practice you work through all the cards and see if you come to the same conclusion.

How many did you find? If you came up with the Sun and only in the right-hand direction, then you have the right answer.

Since Temperance counts onto itself, the count is only from the Sun to Temperance. In the original Ten card spread, the Sun was very popular—*every* card counted onto it. With the addition of Temperance we find that the Sun is isolated. In fact, only one card counts onto the Sun, and that is the Knight of Pentacles!

Catherine's Summary

Elementally, Temperance adds only more Fire; it controls some of the Water, but that's all. It's almost as if she is squaring up to the Water. In a traditional divinatory sense, she comes into her own, she blends the Fire and Water together. If we consider this as aspects of personalities or issues, then she is telling us to work with what we have.

It also reminds me of the old statement that opposites attract, and I think Temperance is showing us how to keep the opposites together.

Paul

How are you doing with the extra card?

Catherine

Obviously you were right about the counting; adding her at the end of the original sequence changes it. I can't see why we would add her to the water or earth string (the Eight of Cups and the Knight of Pentacles) which leaves us with the Fire and the Knight of Wands. This makes more sense, but adding her to the end of a string where the counting has finished feels odd. I think my problem is just in adding her, full-stop. I can see the benefit of adding her after the Sun, because she is the bridge to taming the Fire. The other Knight of Wands string ends with the Four of Cups. It could be said that Temperance is the one holding that cup from the ether, with the elements already blended and ready to go—like a takeaway! It could also be a carrot and stick situation, 'follow me and I'll show you how to blend the opposites'. I feel more like she is a lesson for me, and that instead of choosing another card to extend the reading, it was given anyway.

Queen of Pentacles and Temperance

Now that we have seen what happens when we add a Significator, the Queen of Pentacles, and an extra card, Temperance, it is time to see how the combination of both these cards changes the dynamics of the reading.

Before we analyse this string of cards, it is worth summarising what we have found so far:

- The Knight of Wands in the basic string is entirely ignored by all the cards. However, the Knight connected *to* most of the other cards.

- When we added the Significator, the Queen connected with the Knight, which is progress. The Sun only connected to the Queen of Pentacles and the Knight of Pentacles.

- When we added Temperance, we found that it counted on itself, and only interacted with the Sun.

- In the original String, the Sun connects with every card in both directions—except, of course, the Knight of Wands. With the addition of the Queen of Pentacles or Temperance, suddenly the Sun *only* connects with the Queen and Knight of Pentacles.

- In the basic string, the Eight of Cups connected with all the cards at least once, but when either the Significator or the extra card was introduced, this card became less significant. With the Queen of Pentacles only six cards connected to the Eight of Cups, and when Temperance was included the total was also six cards.

- In the original string, the Knight of Pentacles has a high total, equal to the Sun. When we added the Queen of Pentacles it was not so popular, nor when we added Temperance.

- The Ace of Cups is normally the beginning of love and happiness—in the original spread it is in the position of Hopes and Fears, and all the cards count onto it, which suggests fears more than hope. When we add the Significator, the number of cards it connects to increases slightly.

- We can work through all the cards in this manner to see how the dynamics change. That is the great thing about card counting—it allows us to focus on what is most important in the reading.

Changing the Energies

Take a minute to think about how you would interpret the Queen of Pentacles and Temperance if they were added to a standard Celtic Cross spread. How would you interpret them? Visually, through their pictures? Would you intuitively place them next to one or more of the cards already laid out? Would you see how the energies change and ripple throughout the spread? Which cards benefit from the additions and which ones suffer? Would another Tarot reader agree with you? How would you explain the change?

We have seen how the dynamics of card counting change with the addition of either card. The technique of card counting is consistent and verifiable by anyone who can count. What changes, however, is the interpretation, which will always vary from reader to reader. Next we will look at the further changes that occur when both cards are included in the string.

By now you should be familiar with the principles of card counting, so I will say less about the mechanics and focus more on interpretation.

Queen of Pentacles

The Queen is a good place to start. The first thing we want to know is if she connects to the Knight of Wands. They are not four cards apart, so we will have to go through a few cards to get there.

Counting to the right, we know that she will hit the Sun card, so counting nine we land on Temperance—a good start. Counting twelve takes us to the Knight of Wands! Clearly, the addition of the extra energy is working. Count four and we are on the Ten of Cups, so the energy has gone from fiery to watery, which is confirmed by the Eight of Cups and then back to the Ten of Cups.

Going in the opposite direction takes us on a run of Watery feelings to the Ace of Cups, Four of Cups, Seven of Cups, Ten of Cups and then onto the Fire of Temperance, which takes us back to the Queen again. At last we have a pretty run of cards in both directions which include the Knight of Wands and avoids the Knight of Pentacles.

Temperance

We know that the Queen connects to Temperance, and then to the Knight of Wands, so what happens when we count from Temperance?

I will leave you to work out the details but, counting from the right, Temperance doesn't connect to the Queen, but it does end up on the Ten of Cups, which is a good sign.

When we count from the left, however, the first card is the Queen of Pentacles, then it goes watery with the Four of Cups, Seven of Cups, Ten of Cups, and then finishes where we started, on Temperance.

Temperance is about harmonising and balancing energies, which it seems to do very well, bringing the Knight of Wands and the Queen of Disks together.

The Sun

This card was very significant previously, but now it seems to be ignored by the two extra cards.

The Rules Of Elemental Dignities

Elemental Dignities is a system for uncovering the metaphysical elements (Fire, Air, Water, Earth) in a Tarot spread. It originated within the Golden Dawn magical society, which began in the late Nineteenth Century.

All seventy-eight cards of the Tarot can be associated with one of the four elements. Just as we are attracted or repelled by certain people, so the elements exert a similar effect on each other.

 is attracted to  and

 is attracted to  and

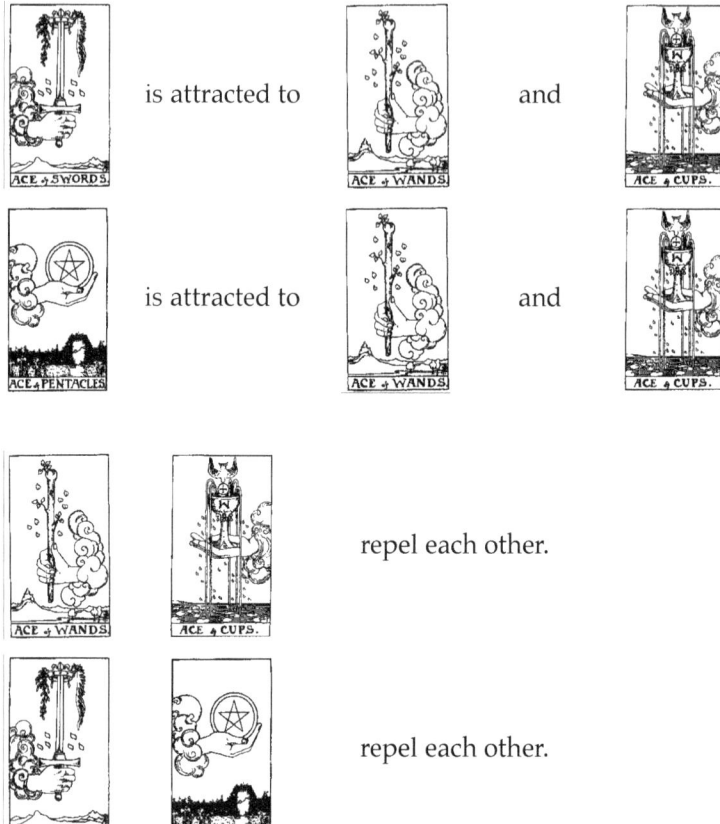

When elements are attracted to each other they become stronger. When they repel they weaken one another. As we can see, there are twice as many laws of attraction as there are of repulsion. To use the system of Elemental Dignities effectively, we need to know a little more about the elements.

    are both *active*.

The Rules Of Elemental Dignities

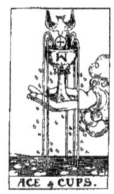  are both *passive*.

Now we can understand better why Fire and Water *don't* work together: Fire is active, whereas Water is passive—they cancel out each other. Similarly, Air and Earth are active and passive respectively, so their energies cancel out each other also. You might wonder, in that case, why Fire and Earth are not repelled by each other, nor Air and Water. The answer is that there is another rule at work, the rule of *friendship*. This becomes apparent when we consider in more detail the qualities of the elements, which we shall examine after the next section.

Pairing The Elements

Using the basic rules of Elemental Dignities, we can draw some conclusions from the permutations of the elements. There are ten permutations of paired elements.

  Fire and Fire is an explosive combination—action on action, so expect some fireworks.

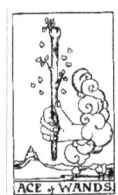 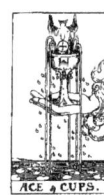 Fire and Water cancel out and weaken each other.

  Fire and Air are friendly and active.

  Fire is active whilst Earth is passive, in which case they are friendly and do not cancel out each other. Instead, they support one another.

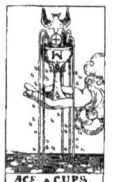  Water with Water is very passive, very still.

  Passive Water with active Air is friendly, so they support each other.

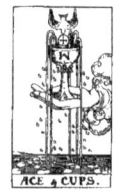  Water and Earth are two passive elements, so do not expect much to change.

  Air with itself is very active.

  Air and Earth is the other inimical combination, so they are weakened and cancel out each other.

  Earth and Earth is an excess of passivity.

Adding Qualities To The Elements

When an element is paired with itself an excess is created, but an excess of what? To answer this question we must add some more qualities to our understanding of each element, namely *temperature* and *moistness*.

  Fire and Fire is a double quantity of heat and dryness.

Fire and Water: hot cancels cold, whilst dry cancels wet.

 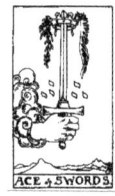
Fire and Air are both hot, but disagree on moistness.

To return to our earlier question of why certain elements are friendly, we can see now that although Fire and Water are completely opposite (as are Air and Earth), the other combinations have something in common:

Fire and Earth are both dry.

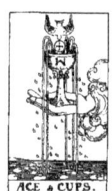 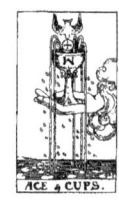
Water and Water is very cold and wet.

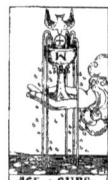 
Water and Air are both wet.

The Rules Of Elemental Dignities

 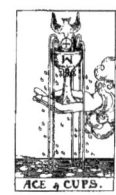 Earth and Water are both cold.

 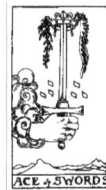 Air and Air is hot and wet. (Think: 'expansion'.)

  Earth and Air: their qualities cancel out each other.

  Earth and Earth is very cold, dry and solid.

CARD PAIRING AND ELEMENTAL DIGNITIES

We do not have to remember the attributions of the paired elements, as long as we are familiar with the rules. The paired elements are building blocks for the bigger picture.

Catherine and I proceeded to use these rules as a basic structure for pairing the cards, putting each pair in the context of the previous pair.

Pairing The Cards

Card Pairing can be done outwards from an individual card in the string, or—more commonly—from the outermost cards to the centre. The technique of Card Pairing includes the rules of Elemental Dignities.

Starting from the outside and working our way inwards:

Eight of Cups Reversed and the Knight of Wands
Catherine
Looking at this pair, I feel slightly different about the Knight than in my previous analysis. I find him gentle and not fiery here, not in this scene. Is he perhaps the one to persuade me not to leave when the going gets tough? Or perhaps he is the one to help me finally turn my back on the past and all my issues and repeated mistakes, and head (with him) to a new future?

Paul
By now we know that the Knight is a future relationship, but the Eight of Cups acts like a hangover.

Seven of Cups and the Ace of Cups
Catherine
So, when we have all these Cups to choose from, what could be more ironic than *another* Cup on offer? I think there is a huge message here. In the past I see that I didn't choose love. I skirted around the issues, either deliberately or blindly. I either did not

choose well or didn't choose at all, judging from those upset Cups on the image of the Eight. I didn't boldly go anywhere, refusing to choose sometimes (Four of Cups), and instead staying safely indoors where life couldn't reach me. I think all these Cups are telling me it's about time I chose life.

Paul

A very passive, watery combination. Looking at this positively, we see the birth of new emotions away from the Seven of Cups.

The Sun and the Ten of Cups
Catherine

The warm vitality of the life-giving sun shining on the happy, contented family in the Ten of Cups. This is what we are really after, the ideal we yearn for. It looks and feels like a blessing and is a choice I would willingly make.

Paul

As Fire and Water these cards conflict, so the positive message of both gets lost.

Three of Swords Reversed and the Ten of Wands
Catherine

I am amazed at how these cards have paired up, more so than the card counting. Looking at these two, we have the pain and we have the pressure, not the best combination, but relevant. Is it coincidental that they paired with each other? The pain is paired with a Knight, or the home directly, or even with new love or apathy. It has gone hand-in-hand with the pressures I experience in balancing my home life. It's the flip side of the previous pair. If I take my rose coloured glasses off, I can see these two lurking around. How related are they? Very, I think, now. There is no doubt the Three relates to my past (and possibly the future), but am I hiding behind my family and home as an excuse not to venture 'out there'?

Paul

Air and Fire are very friendly, so they exacerbate the negative connotations of these cards.

Four of Cups and the Knight of Pentacles
Catherine

What is left to say about these two? The steady reliable Knight of Pentacles combined with the apathy of the Four of Cups. Does this Knight's slower pace affect the Four into slow motion? Though the Knight has many fine qualities, there is nothing going on here, his slower energy is not good for everyone—in contrast to the first pairing where we saw the Knight of Wands actively in pursuit of the Eight of Cups, both cards of movement. But here we have passivity and inertia. I like this pairing less than the previous one. At least we had something to learn there.

Paul

Water and Earth are friendly, but we know the Knight represents a past relationship, making a passive, flat combination.

PAIRING FROM THE QUEEN OF PENTACLES

Adding the Queen of Pentacles at the beginning will change every pairing. There are now eleven cards, so we know there will be one card at the centre.

Queen of Pentacles and Knight of Wands
Catherine

This is the most anticipated pairing, but one I have to assess viewed from the cards and not from within myself. My only concern here is one of balance. Elementally they are neutral, but we do have a difference of ages. Will the Queen be too settled for a younger energetic man?

Paul

Earth and Fire are friendly. She provides the rock, while the Knight adds dynamism.

Eight of Cups and Ace of Cups
Catherine

I see this very much as leaving the past behind and looking ahead to the future with all its potential.

Paul

Two water cards together create a somewhat passive situation. If we see the reversed card as passing, then we have the end of an unhappy emotional situation and the beginning of a new happiness.

Seven of Cups and Ten of Cups

Catherine

The home is a happy place, but the illusion is in how I still miss having a partner yet hide behind the happiness of my family and home so that it doesn't show.

Paul

This combination mirrors the previous pairing, from emotional confusion to more emotional happiness.

Sun and Ten of Wands

Catherine

I like this combination—it makes all that effort seem worthwhile.

Paul

We have switched from two pairs of Water to a pair of Fire. The realisation that emotional happiness is possible suddenly puts on a lot of pressure. Will the new love work? Will Catherine find herself back in the old situation again?

Three of Swords reversed and Knight of Pentacles

Catherine

The sorrow associated with this Knight is one of loss. It was an important relationship.

Paul

Here is what she fears, sorrow from the previous man, but we can also see this as her leaving him behind in favour of the new man, once she knows the new relationship can work. Air and Earth are inimical, which exacerbates the situation.

Four of Cups
Catherine

I would not want this card to be so important here, but I continue to receive its message—though you have to wonder how apathy could develop with a fiery knight. Forewarned is forearmed, as they say.

Paul

To some extent, until the new man arrives and she can leave her ex behind, Catherine is unable to move completely forward. Water is friendly with the previous pairing of Air and Earth, which suggests things will improve.

Summary
Catherine

The pairings were encouraging in this set, even the ones that looked negative initially. The Three of Swords was paired where I think it belonged, in the past and with my ex-partner. Closely linked to that is the Eight of Cups, who is in turn finding the Ace, just over the hill. The Four of Cups is the only card to remain in the negative, not having a partner in this pairing. It seems to be a fundamental issue in my life.

Paul

Pairing the cards with the Queen of Pentacles shows that progress can be made. When we were card counting, the Knight of Wands was always elusive, but now he is firmly in the picture.

Pairing With Temperance

We placed Temperance at the opposite end to the Queen of Pentacles, so again the pairings are different.

Eight of Cups reversed and Temperance
Catherine

I see here that Temperance would be attempting to persuade the man in the Eight of Cups not to leave, but to work it out.

Paul

Fire and Water cancel each other out. If we consider reversed cards to be 'weaker', then Temperance is the stronger card, so there is a little bit of fiery energy to move the situation forward.

Seven of Cups and Knight of Wands reversed

Catherine

Well, we just have to ask: is this going to be a good idea? Will this man be a bad influence on me and therefore on my life? Is the whole scenario an illusion, or is the basis of the relationship in question?

Paul

Temperance is about harmonising opposing energies and so far we have had two pairings of Fire and Water. It would seem that Catherine has a lot of doubts about whether she can handle new love in her life.

Sun and Ace of Cups

Catherine

After the questionable pairing of the previous two, we have such a wonderful pair here. It could not get any better than this, could it?

Paul

Fire and Water continue to pair! Since Aces are about the beginning of the element, the Sun card is very strong, almost overpowering.

Three of Swords reversed and Ten of Cups

Catherine

Unhappiness and sorrow associated with the home. This is not pleasant for me to look at, but even I know that a subtle shift can cause a huge difference.

Paul

At last a different element, Air, which suggests doubts about keeping the family happy. But still, Air and Water are friendly.

Four of Cups and Ten of Wands
Catherine

This one stands to reason; the daily grind is not anything to get excited about. But it does show why we look for comfort or excitement from outside sources.

Paul

Back to Water and Fire again. The passive nature of the Four is weakened by the Ten. We feel the weight, with no way to release the pressure.

Knight of Pentacles
Catherine

Temperance would most definitely have helped the relationship with this Knight, but it belongs in the past. Its lesson is to apply it to the future.

Paul

Temperance is about blending and harmonising energies, but here, we see that in comparison to the addition of the Queen of Pentacles, the pairing brings nothing but problems. The message is clear: Catherine needs to put her needs first, then she can find happiness and success in relationships.

Summary
Catherine

The most interesting pairing for me was the Seven of Cups and the Knight of Wands. I hadn't questioned whether this Knight was an honourable man or not; I had expected it to be so. The potential exists in everyone to act questionably from time to time, but it is important to heed the lesson from these two together.

Overall, the pairings seem a little disjointed and sometimes extreme. The aim is the Sun and the Ace. The reality is the rest of the pairings, which represent real life and what we have to work hard at.

Pairing The Queen Of Pentacles And Temperance

The final set of pairings includes both extra cards. This section is very short, and the reason is obvious if you think about it. The

Queen and Temperance start the pairing and from then onwards we have exactly the same pairings that we started with.

Catherine

I initially looked at this and thought Temperance would have no work to do here. There is no Fire or Water here, and we are dealing with a Queen and not a fiery Knight. This, though, is a narrow-minded view. No one is perfect and we should all be looking to improve ourselves and harmonise with our environments and the people in our lives.

Temperance is working directly with the Queen in this situation, rather like a therapist. The Queen has Temperance's undivided attention, so now is the time to work out any issues that require her assistance.

Paul

Earth and Fire are perfectly compatible, and they strengthen elements that are weak and under-represented in this reading.

Pairing From Other Cards

It is perfectly possible to pair from any card in the sequence. As an exercise, try pairing from the Knights using the basic sequence, then with the Queen of Pentacles added, then with Temperance added, then with both of them.

Analysing Three-Card Combinations

In the previous section we looked how the elements interacted when there were two cards, using Pairing. Now it is time to look at how the elements interact when there are three cards. With this knowledge we can analyse each card relative to its neighbours.

Fire and Water

Fire and Water are enemies, so they fight and weaken each other.

 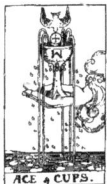 

Fire is active and hot, whereas Water is passive and cold. In this combination Water is devastated, dried up, desiccated. Here we have super-heated steam without mass (Earth) or intelligence (Air). Thesis and Antithesis act together blindly (no Air) and without durability (Earth) to destroy Synthesis.

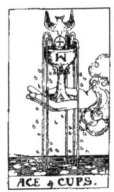  

Now the situation is reversed. The Fire is extinguished by Water. Any activity is swamped. The emotions overcome any actions, creating stagnation because there is no Air, but the lack of Earth provides no

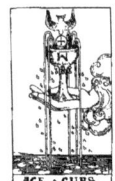

basis to the feelings so there is an expansion but without any kind of structure.

The Principal (in the middle) has support from one Moderator. There is still no intelligent control, or a strong basis from either Air or Earth. We have a flammable liquid here. Looked at from another perspective, since the Moderators are enemies, they actually have a neutral effect on the situation, so the action goes ahead with nothing to enhance or retard it, but does not last long (no endurance from Earth), and lacks any kind of direction (Air).

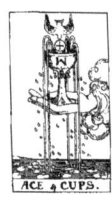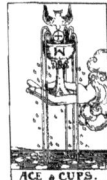

The Principal is supported by one Moderator. The Moderators do not work together. The two Water aspects gang up to prevent any action taking place—or, to put it another way, since the Moderators have an overall neutral effect, the natural tendency of water to inertia would suggest that nothing will actually happen, since there is no mental stimulation, but the effect will gradually spread as it is not contained. (No Earth.)

AIR AND EARTH

Air and Earth are mutual enemies, like Fire and Water, but the effect is very different.

 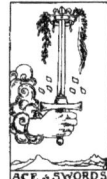 

This is intelligence destroyed in ignorance. The absence of Fire and Water indicates no change, energy, or any kind of emotion. In fact there could be a leeching of any kind of energy as the Earth elements work together to drain away the Air element, perhaps by passive resistance.

This situation is analogous to a cretin amongst a company of intellectuals. The simpleton has no comprehension of the ideas or communications around him. Since Earth-types seek security, there would be great fear here, as Air is the most unstable of the elements. An appropriate image would be a ping-pong ball hovering and bouncing around in a jet of air.

In the next two examples Synthesis triumphs as Thesis and Antithesis go to war.

 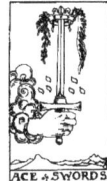 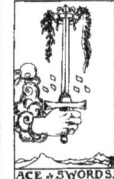

The Air cards triumph and are smug about their intellectual achievements, but there is doubt over the usefulness of the victory. It is like a Lawyer arguing and winning an obscure point of law that is lost on the jury.

An intellectual ranting, failing to stir the complacent security of Earth. There is no point of contact, no emotive sensation of togetherness such as Water might bring to the situation, nor any kind of movement or change. This is a thinker who is trapped in a hopeless situation. Brain-power will not achieve anything, and there is no energy (Fire), nor any point in trying to engage the emotions or use some kind of seductive strategy.

FIRE AND AIR

These two elements are both active and friendly to each other, so the problems arise from the lack of basis (Earth) or feeling (Water), in which case there will be little comfort or security in the experience. While Air will provide intelligence to actions, there will be over-exuberance at the least, and obsessive behaviour at worst. The results will either be burn-out or some kind of confrontation. Since Air is such an antagonistic and divisive element, the differences between Thesis and Antithesis are heightened, even when they are friendly or of the same element. In some of the examples below, we see an unholy alliance developing.

This is an interesting combination. Thesis and Antithesis combine to create some kind of intelligence, but it will have a low kind of cunning, and is destined to continuous action, rather than the periods of introspection that thinking requires from time to time. This might also represent someone coerced to reveal thought

processes due to violent pressure, perhaps under torture.

Two opposing thought processes result in spontaneous action. A train of events is set in action, but there is no possibility of considered change as a result of new circumstances. This indicates a mediation process that breaks down, resulting in war, either physical or verbal. Another alternative is active blame or an attack on a third party to cover up ideological differences—the rise of Fascism; blaming weak ethnic groups for problems arising in society as a whole and using them as an excuse for totalitarian behaviour.

Action is inspired by a combination of thought and action without lust for the result. This is a wavering intellectual forced or inspired to action. This example and the next are far more desirable than the previous two, but there are still problems due to the lack of Water and Earth.

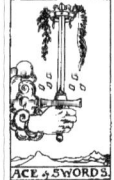

Fire tries (but probably fails, ultimately) to inspire Air to action. If Air does act, the outcome will be inherently unstable or vacillating as soon as the pressure is removed. There is no respite in this relentless combination.

Water and Earth

Like Fire and Air, these elements are compatible and friendly but they are also completely passive and therefore sloth and turpitude are a problem. Moist Earth is fertile, but the spark of life is required. As before, there are four basic combinations. Since Earth is involved we can introduce some topography into the descriptions. Without Fire, these events might therefore be considered to be happening 'at night'. In the first two examples, Thesis and Antithesis fail to find any difference between themselves but nevertheless conspire to swamp the result.

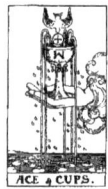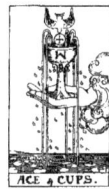

This is an island amidst cold icy seas, bleak and uninhabitable under a full moon. There is no wind of course (Air), so no waves. This is a ship stationary on calm waters; water vapour condensing into snow or ice; vegetation under the water. Emotions and feelings have solidified, but there is still a lack of activity. This can represent a sinking into depression.

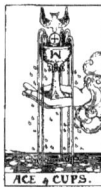

This is a lake or slow-moving river, possibly iced over. It represents a slight fluidity in a solidly packed situation, like an underground river; a stagnant spring that fails to fertilise the land around it; a pocket of crude oil hidden underground; or an aquifer. Here we see the leaching away of any kind of emotional experience under the dead weight of insensitivity. Earth mops up Water. This is the emotional identification with and eventual subsuming by the Earth.

In this and the next example Thesis and Antithesis are different, but change comes about through inertia or a kind of osmosis due to a difference of pressure.

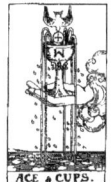  

We could see this combination as a straining, while below the lees remain. It is like high-tide at the seaside.

This is a drying out or a mopping up, but not due to aeration or heat. It is the solidification of a viscous liquid, a heavy weight or a situation that squeezes out all feelings into numbness.

FIRE AND EARTH

Fire and Earth are friendly to each other, but whereas Fire is all action Earth is totally passive. Consequently, the impression is either of arrival or departure.

Here we see the purification or tempering of a substance through fire. The result would be ash, clinker, or a refined material. Usually, heated substances liquidise or vaporise into the air, but as there is no Air here we cannot determine this. Alternatively, it represents opposing actions resulting in karmic consequences; forces overwhelmingly imposed on a stationary object; or an object projected upwards.

This situation is precisely the opposite of the example above. The stationary pressures of Earth around Fire suggests a volcano, or hot gases venting from the ground. Since Thesis and Antithesis are represented by Earth, we might view this as a chemical or nuclear reaction resulting from a critical mass being reached with a release of heat energy.

Movement plus inertia results in action; a conflagration that destroys Earth but continues burning as it uses up its fuel.

Movement plus inertia results in a substance that is warm, suggesting some kind of a chemical reaction. Maybe critical mass is not reached, but we arrive at a stable situation that has a degree of life.

AIR AND WATER

These elements are friendly to each other, but both are unstable, lacking structure. Air is active, whilst Water is passive.

 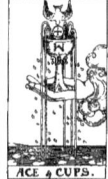 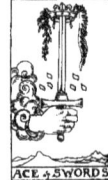

A cloud or water droplets in the air. The lack of earth suggests that the cloud is hovering. There would be no heat, so maybe we are looking here at snow or hail. The absence of Earth shows that there would be no structure, form or stability. The action of two different gases has created another gas with greater weight. Arguments and contrary ideas somehow create an emotional response.

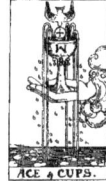

An air-bubble suspended in Water. This is an intellectual impulse arising out of conflicting emotional experiences. It has some definition, maybe due to the pressure of the water, but is probably not going anywhere. It is the desire to rise out of an overwhelming emotional situation, perhaps by removing the emotions and replacing them with logic.

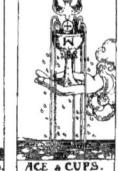

Thesis and Antithesis are at work to remove feeling from emotions and arrive at mental clarity.

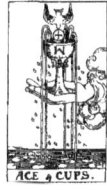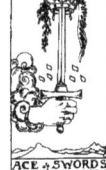

Water and the emotions win out over the thought processes. Here we have dreams, fantasies and a total lack of reality.

Advanced Elemental Analysis And Elemental Bases

So far we have looked at the bigger picture of the string of cards by working through the Card Counting from the Eight of Cups, Knight of Disks and Knight of Wands, and pairing the cards from outside to centre and from other cards. We have also counted and paired after adding the Queen of Pentacles and Temperance in order to increase our understanding of what is happening in Catherine's life.

All these methods give us an overview. It is now time to go into even greater detail on how individual cards interact with each other. To do this we use the rules of Elemental Dignities to understand the relative strengths and weaknesses of each triplet. The centre card of each triplet is the focus.

It's so easy to learn the rules of Elemental Dignities you'll find that as you card count you will automatically factor in the subtleties of the elemental analysis.

All seventy-eight cards can be associated with one of the four elements, therefore it does not matter if the card is Major, Minor, or a Court Card; we can analyse it in relationship to any other cards using the rules of Elemental Dignities:

- Fire (Wands) and Water (Cups) weaken each other.
- Air (Swords) and Earth (Pentacles) weaken each other.

That is basically all you need to remember! Using the rules of logic, and adding a few qualities such as 'active' and 'passive' we can deduce the other rules.

Catherine had already studied Elemental Dignities on my web site before she contacted me. Once I had answered a few of her questions we both produced our analysis of the cards taking into account the Elemental Dignities. As you will see, although the rules of Elemental Dignities are unambiguous, interpretations will differ. We are factoring in also the context of the reading, the Querent, the position with respect to Pairing and Card Counting, and the divinatory meanings of the cards themselves.

With practice, a natural 'commentary' will develop that condenses and contains all of these factors. However, in the commentaries below, we will 'think aloud' to demonstrate how we came to our conclusions.

We start with the Eight of Cups. On one side of it will be the card from the other end, the Knight of Wands reversed. On the other side is the Seven of Cups.

Eight Cups reversed

Catherine

The Seven of Cups is the strongest card and although it is at odds with Fire, it is buffered by the principal. Fire is in trouble and completely overrun by Water, making this a passive situation.

Paul

The Water cards overpower the Knight of Wands, who is marginalised.

Seven of Cups

Catherine

The Eight of Cups is the strongest card. Only one moderator supports the principal and both moderators cancel each other out. This is a passive situation, the Water cancelling out the action of the Fire, despite the Fire coming from the strongest source, the Sun. We have no logic or stability here.

Paul

This combination is the same as for the Eight of Cups, so again the fire of the Sun card is very weak.

The Sun

Catherine

The Three of Swords is the strongest card. Fire is supported by the Air but weakened by the Water. The moderators are friendly to each other and so become stronger than our principal card. Interestingly, with respect to divinatory meaning the Sun would be dominant here, but elementally it is struggling. Although we have some thought and mental activity, we still do not have any stability —in fact, we potentially have a volatile situation.

Paul

The Sun takes strength from the Air of the Three of Swords, but is weakened by the Seven of Cups. The Seven of Cups passively supports the Air. Since neither are very happy cards, the Sun is weaker, while the Three of Swords is strengthened.

Three of Swords

Catherine

The Three of Swords wins again. It is actively supported by the Fire while the Water is neutral and passive. The moderators are enemies and therefore strengthen the Air further. The Sun is slightly stronger here too as although it is an enemy of the other moderator, it is not being directly affected by it.

Paul

The Three of Swords is friendly with Water and Fire, so it gains strength. We can consider Air to be a child of Fire and Water. Overall, this combination is active.

Four of Cups

Catherine

The Four of Cups is the strongest card. The Water is supported by passive Earth, and the active Air is neutral. No one is an enemy here; both the moderators are neutral. Though we have stability, our problem now is one of inertia despite the activity of the Air. It could make our Water a bit choppy, but it will be settled by the Earth.

Paul

The Four of Cups is the strongest card as it is friendly with Air and Earth. The surrounding elements fight each other. This combination is more passive than active.

Knight of Pentacles
Catherine

The Knight is the strongest here. It is supported by the Water and is neutral with the Fire. This is another passive situation. Despite the Fire, the Earth prevents any activity. We also have Air missing, so there is no thinking our way out of this.

Paul

The Knight is the strongest here, but the overall energy is passive—he does not want to get out of his comfort zone.

Ten of Wands
Catherine

The Knight wins again. Water is an enemy of the Fire, while the Fire is neutral to the Earth. Both moderators are friendly to each other. Fire has no Air to feed it—another stuck situation—but the moderators, despite their passivity, are comfortable. The Fire reduces to a flame.

Paul

The Knight is strongest as he is friendly with Water and Fire, but again he will not act unless pushed.

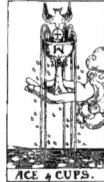

Ten of Cups

Catherine

The Ace is the strongest. We have a repeat of the beginning triplet; the Fire is being extinguished by the Water. Its problems will not be difficult to overcome, though the absence of stability and logic can cause the emotions to overrun.

Paul

The Ace is the strongest. This combination is similar to the Seven of Cups and Eight of Cups. We can see the glimmer of the hope for change, but remember that this is a passive combination, so do not expect change very quickly.

Ace of Cups

Catherine

The Ten of Cups wins this last battle. The moderators are at odds and only one of them are supporting the principal card. It has been a familiar scenario in this spread, Water dominating Fire with the absence of Earth and Air. It is interesting to note that with this triplet and the previous one, the principal was demoted to the sidelines and the moderator of the same element was the strongest card. This shows the influence of the other cards present and the interaction between them.

Paul

Another similar combination. The Knight is rebelling against the two Water cards, but where is his energy?

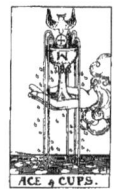

Knight of Wands reversed
Catherine

The Knight is the last in our sequence, so we will add the first card, the Eight of Cups to the end to form a triplet. Once again the Fire is in trouble, surrounded by all that Water. Any action brought by this card is swamped by the passivity of the others.

Paul

The Knight is very weak, surrounded as he is by Water.

QUEEN OF PENTACLES AS SIGNIFICATOR

Eight of Cups reversed
Catherine

Earth as an island and overrun by the Water. Excessively emotional.

Queen of Pentacles

Catherine

The Queen of Pentacles is strongest and comfortable. Though we are lacking thought or rationale, we do have the action and emotion which is grounded.

Paul

The Queen of Pentacles surrounded by the reversed Eight of Cups and Knight of Wands is friendly to both. Maybe she feels like a fish out of water.

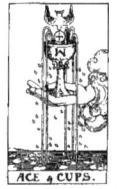

Knight of Wands reversed

Catherine

The Queen reigns supreme again. The Knight of Wands is weakened by the Water of the Ace, but the Queen is supported by it. Once again she grounds and stabilises.

Summary

Catherine

I previously saw myself as the figure in the Eight of Cups, doing the walking. Now that my Significator, the Queen of Pentacles, has been added to the layout, I can see my involvement. I realise now that before I was a spectator, viewing from a safe point. By adding the Queen to the cards I am now an active player. It seems ludicrous to say that, because this is of course, my life, but I just had not viewed it that way. I now see the Eight of Cups as an action and not as myself.

Temperance As An Extra Card

Eight of Cups reversed
Catherine

We have Water dominating now, like an ocean. Here we have excessive passivity.

Temperance
Catherine
Fire still running amok.

Knight of Wands reversed
Catherine

Fire dominates. There is much passion here, but nothing to keep it in check.

Summary

Catherine

Elementally Temperance only adds more Fire, which controls some of that Water but that is all. It's almost as if she is squaring up to the Water. In a traditional divinatory sense, she comes into her own, she blends the Fire and Water together. If we consider this as an aspect of personalities or issues, then she is telling us to work with what we have. It also reminds me of the old statement that opposites attract and I think Temperance is showing us how to keep the opposites together.

Paul

Temperance surrounded by the reversed Eight of Cups and the Knight of Wands has a fiery imbalance, but at least this provides energy to move out of the current situation.

QUEEN OF PENTACLES AND TEMPERANCE

Queen of Pentacles

Catherine

The Queen wins, in a triplet with action, emotion and stability.

Temperance

Catherine

Fire is spreading with nothing to stop it. Earth is friendly to it and so won't stand in its way.

Paul

The Earth and Fire of the Queen and Temperance bring practicality and energy to the situation.

Summary

Catherine

We have three identical triplets with two Water elements and one Fire. This makes me wonder how much I push the passion away, or at least the thought of it. If I do not join in I cannot possibly be hurt, but I will never know if I might have been happy.

Paul

Whenever the energy of Fire tries to do something it is either weakened or sabotaged by Water. There are two other combinations, in particular the Sun, which takes energy from the Air of the Three of Swords, so maybe it is the thoughts of sorrow and separation that fuel change.

ELEMENTAL BASES

The sequence of cards can be further analysed by placing it in turn on the elemental bases of Fire, Water, Air and Earth. Using the rules of Elemental Dignities, the element of each card interacts with the base as well as the cards on either side of it.

When we analyse the cards according to the elemental bases, we apply special meanings to each base:

- Fire—the past.
- Water—emotions and desires.
- Air—problems and worries.
- Earth—the future, the outcome.

This technique is illustrated in the interpretations below.

Fire—Past

Catherine

The Water cards are not doing well with Fire as the base. Relating that to the past, and the relative strengths of the Fire and Air cards, we see the Water cards in a secondary role. They are the by-product of the unstable activity around the Sun and the Three of Swords. Further down the string, and wedged between the Ten and Knight of Wands, we have two more Water cards, seemingly in trouble. This is the first time I have looked at these cards from the perspective of the past. To me, they represent the present and the future, so it is a little difficult. However, facing it head-on, and acknowledging how the past affects the future, then it seems that we can see how fragile our dreams can be. With all that Fire around, our Water cards are in danger of evaporating. So, standing here in the present, looking at the future through the eyes of the past, I am looking for the reason why my hopes and dreams may be in trouble, and I can look no further than the other Fire card—the Sun —and the sentimentality I have held in the past.

Paul

The Fire cards will be excessive, while Water really struggles. This string of cards shows the difficulties of the past. There is only one Air card, and it gains energy from the Fire, but since it is the Three of Swords, we do not expect good thoughts or ideas, or an easy time in relationships.

Water—Desires & Passions

Catherine

My eye is led to three cards very much in trouble—the Fire cards. Looking at those first and remembering that Water deals with passions and desires, I cannot help but be concerned for the Knight of Wands. Is this suggesting that this person in my future is not someone whom I desire? Or at least, not to begin with. This would be another confirmation of the strings leading from the Knight that suggested perhaps a friendship first and a romance later. This doesn't look so bad, so what about the other Fire cards? Considering the hard work represented in the Ten of Wands, it would be manageable on this base. Looking at it like this is reassuring. The Sun seems somewhat problematic, but if I actually think back to the Eight of Cups and how I turned my back on love, then it would be acceptable to say that I have had no desire or passion for it. I like it that the Cups are strong, but of course I am less impressed by the others. I cannot ignore them though, as they have represented how I have felt, and how I have handled things previously. I still have a lot of thinking to do, which has to begin with the Knight of Pentacles. He dominates all the strings, but invariably ends in loops. He is very attractive to me, but wholly wrong for me at the same time.

Paul

We have an excess of Water cards, which makes the entire string very dreamy and passive. The Fire cards are further weakened. The solitary Air card, the Three of Swords, will go along with Water, while the practicality of Earth is diminished.

Air—Problems
Catherine

Except for the Knight of Pentacles, all the cards are elementally sound. This I find interesting as we are looking now at the realm of problems. So what does that say? Well, at first glance all looks well, until we examine the strong cards, and now I can see that all is not well at all. It is no surprise to see the Sun, the Three of Swords and the Ten of Wands strong in the base of Air. It has been well-established how the Sun and the Three of Swords have been issues in my past, and how the Ten of Wands is a present trouble. What is worrying is the two Knights. Since I am backing the Knight of Wands as my future Prince Charming, it is not reassuring to see him as a problem. On the flip side, I have the Knight of Pentacles weak in the base of Air. Now this would at first seem to be a contradiction, and definitely not the desired result, but the counting with the Knight of Wands showed a potential problem at the beginning of a relationship, so this actually confirms that.

Paul

There is only one Air card, the Three of Swords, so the focus will be on relationships. The Fire cards are strengthened, but through the Air card, which tends to aggrandise the situation.

Earth—Future Outcome

Catherine

The Water cards look to have the validity now, a base supporting them. Does that make them more realistic, or does it settle them down? There is much passivity here. The Three of Swords is in trouble, which is a relief for the future. Interesting that the Knight of Pentacles is ruling this, considering I had decided the future was not with him. In fact, I cannot take my eyes off him; he seems like a concrete block in the middle there—like a milestone. The Sun looks interesting because as the principle card in its triplet, it doesn't fare too well. The Three of Swords has been weakened by the Earth and so is not supporting the Sun now. Supported by the Earth, the Water is stronger and putting a lot of pressure on the Sun. Looking at the other end of the sequence, the other Fire cards are less effective. The Ten and Knight of Wands are anchored in the inertia of the Water and Earth around them. They have not been extinguished, but they certainly seem to have been tamed.

Paul

This is the strongest configuration for these cards, as the Earth base supports the excess of Water, mopping it up. Fire is also supported as it gains energy from the Earth.

The Transforming Power Of The Aces

The Aces represent the origins of the four elements. In Eastern philosophy, *Akasha* or 'Space' precedes the creation of the four elements, which gives us five elements in total. This is the reason we count *five* for the Aces. Each Ace represents the transformation from Space or Akasha into its element. There are times in a reading when things feel 'stuck'. When this happens, Tarot readers really do have an ace up their sleeve!

From Akasha the four elements emanate, so when we count from an Ace—for instance, the Ace of Cups—we are seeing how its element (Water, in this case) spreads through the cards. We use a combination of Card Counting and Elemental Dignities to explore the results. From the Ace of Cups we would naturally expect the Water element to emerge, but if the spread is stuck we have the possibility of another element appearing. Naturally, the count will have to change to effect this, so instead of five we use *eleven*, a powerful spiritual number.

In Catherine's spread there is only one Ace, of Cups, which simplifies things somewhat. First we will count five with the basic cards, then we will count eleven to see what changes. Then we will do the same, except with the addition of the Queen of Pentacles, then Temperance, and finally both cards together.

Not all combinations will 'work', of course, but we now have options we didn't have before.

Card Counting The Basic Ten Cards

Ace as Five

The Ace nestles between the Ten of Cups, representing home and family, and the Knight of Wands reversed, the new man who has not yet appeared. As the Aces are the root or beginnings of an element, the rules of Elemental Dignities do not apply so much, so the fiery energy of the Knight is not as much of a problem as you might think. The Ace of Cups is a sign that Catherine's new love will work on a personal as well as a family level.

When we count five to the right we go to the Sun, another positive card, and then the Ten of Cups. So far, so good. Things then become problematic. The sequence goes on to the Ten of Wands, the Knight of Pentacles, and finally back to the Ace. It seems that Catherine has problems getting started, because although the first few cards are good, we find ourselves back onto old patterns. When we start and finish on the same card, there is a short circuit going on. The situation is stillborn.

Counting in the other direction is depressing. We begin with the Four of Cups, the Seven of Cups, the Knight of Pentacles, the Sun, and back to the Four of Cups, which is hardly the most dynamic card in the Tarot!

Ace as Eleven

If there are ten cards, and the count is for eleven, what will be the result? We will start and finish on the same card! The Ace of Cups exists in splendid isolation—it knows only itself. But when we add an extra card we will have a different scenario.

Adding The Queen Of Pentacles

Ace as Five

I will leave you to work out the exact path in both directions. The result is the same in both cases—we arrive back on the Ace.

Ace as Eleven

When we count eleven we arrive on the cards next to the Ace, the Ten of Cups and the Knight of Wands—a good start, but things peter out quickly, because we end on (guess what?) the Ace of Cups.

Adding Temperance

A little thought will tell us that since the Ace of Cups did not count onto the Queen of Pentacles, the outcome is going to be no different with Temperance. So we can proceed to the final example: card counting with both the Queen *and* Temperance.

The Queen And Temperance

Ace as Five

Counting to the right we begin with Eight of Cups, which is not particularly inspiring. Next is the Ten of Cups, then the Four of Cups, which takes us back to the Ten of Cups. So here is Catherine's alternative, simply finding happiness within the family. All the cards are watery and therefore passive. Counting to the left is more interesting, particularly as both the Queen and Temperance are part of the count. However, we end on the Ace again.

Ace as Eleven

Remarkably, whichever direction we go, we find ourselves back on the Ace. Counting left includes both the Queen and Temperance, just as it did when we counted five.

Summary

What have we learned from this? Catherine finds it very difficult to make a new start. Unfortunately, we do not have another Ace in the spread to see what other differences could be made.

Catherine's Interpretation

Counting with the Queen of Pentacles—Aces Count Five

Initially it felt a little discomforting to see the Eight of Cups and the Three of Swords dominating by their absence. If they are the source then what am I to do? Looking at the next two cards, the Queen of Pentacles and the Knight of Wands, I have to wonder if they are the key to making this better. Seeing as the Queen is myself and the Knight my future love-interest, then I would like to say we can change the direction of the Nile. What I must remember is that the Eight and the Three are reversals and so not fully expressed, which is a relief. I should also bear in mind that, as the source, they will be where I am coming from, and not necessarily where I am going to.

I've never been very good at choosing, so to be given all those choices is somewhat ironic. But if I look historically to my past relationship with the Knight of Pentacles, then it becomes the most appropriate card in the world! With the Ace of Cups, it represents all the times I thought about going back to that relationship. Many times I did, but like the loops and circles in the counting, it's what happened in reality. It has been the most well-trodden path for me. The two Tens exist as they do in life, but breaking the cycles and loops is the key.

Counting with the Queen of Pentacles—Aces Count Eleven

With the Ten and Ace of Cups receiving the most hits, translating to the most trodden path, it seems appropriate to link new love with the happy home life. I actually don't leave the house much, and it was the scene for my relationship with the Knight of Pentacles and also my marriage, so that could justify its presence here with the Ace.

Perhaps one of the keys to breaking those cycles and loops lies with a change of scenery so that love can come, I have joked about 'leaving the house' to find someone new. There seems to be a lot of irony in these cards! One way to step out of the loop is to literally get out there!

Counting with Temperance—Aces Count Five

Some things never change. Though the appearance of the Sun is interesting, because previously it was shown to represent sentimentality and the past. But here it is at the source and so it's encouraging, lightening the darker cards.

Counting with Temperance—Aces Count Eleven

What strikes me as odd with this set is how the cards have either a lot or very little hits in the counting; only the two Knights are lingering in the middle. The usual suspects are here, but this time we have the Ten of Wands showing up. This isn't strange as it has gone hand-in-hand with the Ten of Cups in the main counting.

Counting with the Queen and Temperance—Aces Count Five

It is interesting that the Three of Swords and the Ten of Cups are both out on their own in terms of hits. They feature in the extreme as they are also what we have experienced and what we desire. Remembering that the Three is reversed and so not fully expressed is a help, but we must also remind ourselves of its meaning. At the source, once again, I can only hope that we lead back to the happy home I desire in the Ten of Cups, but this time with the Knight of Wands.

Counting with the Queen and Temperance—Aces Count Eleven

This hasn't happened before. We have a new card leading the way as the source but, interestingly, it is a card that has appeared in the statistics for the most hits on previous counts—the Seven of Cups. I like it here though, not just because it replaces the cards that bothered me most, the Eight of Cups and the Three of Swords, but because it offers so many choices. This is the first time I have felt positive about all those choices. I can only see it as a good thing at the source. It says to me that there are a myriad of possibilities and many doors are open. Couple that with the Sun, and it all seems bright and happy, with the choices being all mine. I am in control. No matter how dark things may sometimes appear, I know I have other choices I can make.

The Ten of Cups is a familiar player here and there isn't much left to say except it is where I would like to be. Even though it is the most trodden path, it is still my desire to achieve domestic happiness. Of course, having a Knight on my arm would be the icing on the cake.

Looking at how many times the Ace counts back onto itself, it makes me wonder if I will always be looking for love. In some ways I can translate that to always looking for something better, akin to the grass being greener. I have actually done this in my life, so the Ace counting back on itself is a true reflection of how my love-life has been: the apathy, the sorrow, the leaving and the moving on to pastures new. It's actually part of the process that has been identified in other cards, but until now has not been identified with this one. And so the lessons continue.

Summary

The question now must be, how do I find permanency? Immediately I think of Temperance and her pairing with the Queen of Pentacles in the final counting. I saw her acting as a therapist to the Queen there, so bringing that option to this situation has the potential to end at least one of those cycles I have been a part of for so long. This now gives me three options:

1. I do nothing and let the cycles continue, hoping that change will come all by itself or from somewhere as yet unidentified.

2. I seek out an actual therapist and work out my issues that way.

3. I continue to use the Tarot as the wonderful tool for learning and transformation that it has so far been for me.

This has been the most productive part of the exercise. Instead of just identifying a problem, I now have a potential solution. This is very encouraging and is of course something I will explore now that I have a direction in which to go.

Uncounted Cards: The Magic Of Tarot

The spiritual realms by definition are invisible—we often detect their absence in our life by loneliness, sorrow or isolation. The yearning we all experience, even if we cannot articulate it, is within us all, particularly when we are looking for a partner, someone to share our life with. Beyond a soul-mate, the ultimate relationship is with our Spiritual aspects. However, as we have trouble dealing with people who are flesh and blood, how much more difficult will it be for our Spiritual Nature? With Catherine our efforts went into finding new love, but what happened was a growth in spiritual knowledge and insight. Used correctly, the Tarot helps us to connect to our Source. When we discover the uncounted cards in a spread we begin to see a trickle of water bubble up in the dry river bed, and as we track the cards that follow from the uncounted cards, the trickle increases in volume, bringing life, fertility, and growth in the river and onto the banks as the water flows towards the ocean. When we see the flow from source to goal, we have uncovered the hidden story of past, present and future.

To be truly uncounted, a card has to have no card counting onto it from either direction. From the uncounted card itself we can count in either direction. As we have seen, adding a card, or changing the count from the Aces to eleven from five changes the dynamics of the reading. Clearly, we will also see uncounted cards change as a result.

Uncounted cards can represent aspects of a situation of which the client may well be unaware. We have all had a reading where things seem so clear to us, but the look on the client's face tells us that she has no idea what we are talking about. Then again, there are times when neither the reader nor the client understands what a particular card is about. Uncounted cards can also be about the future. Confusing? Not really. Something that is not known currently may well soon appear in the future. Forewarned is forearmed. If the cards associated with the uncounted card are not favourable, it would be an idea to see if we can move away from future danger. Conversely, if the omens are good, we might look forward.

Uncounted cards tell us where things are not fixed. They indicate fluidity and flexibility, and so we can change the outcome to our advantage. If we intend to change the outcome we need to know more about what is going on. We need to know the nature and number of cards that emanate from the uncounted cards. If there is more than one uncounted card, we want to know how close the string of cards come to each other. We also need to know the Elemental Dignities of the uncounted cards. Armed with this information, we are then in a position to consider magical rituals, because various kinds of spirits are associated with the Tarot cards.

When I was working and studying the string of cards that were the basis for my book *Tarot and the Magus* I became very aware of the subtleties and nuances of the energies as they moved through and transformed the reading. After spending over two months working on the same cards, spirits spontaneously appeared to me in a very friendly way, offering to help. Working with Elemental Dignities and Card Counting, it seems that the reader is harmonised with the energies that ebb and flow in time. This resonance creates a stronger link to the spiritual forces embedded within the cards. These spiritual forces also strengthen the reader, creating the opportunity for greater wisdom and knowledge to develop.

In a nutshell, instead of having to work out which spiritual forces to work with, the Tarot itself will tell the alert reader what needs to be done, or which spirit to work with. By combining the techniques of Card Counting, Elemental Dignities and Pairing, we initiate the process of change that happens within the time of the reading. The client becomes more confident, assured or inspired. Equipped with new insights they can face the future with confidence.

SPIRITUAL POINTERS

Working with the spiritual forces associated with the Tarot is a specialist subject. Few Tarot readers feel comfortable with such a notion, and it is easy to see why. However, as long as you take a balanced view of the Tarot, it is unlikely that you will encounter any problems.

Having said that, there are a couple of points I would like to make. First, we are not talking about 'magical spells'. In my experience they do not work. These kinds of things antagonise our base instincts and are ultimately self-defeating.

In general, the spiritual powers associated with the Tarot can be broken down into three distinct groups:

1. Major Arcana—see: Crowley's *Liber 231*.
2. Minor Arcana (but not the Aces)—see: The Goetia.
3. Court Cards and Aces—see: Enochian Magic.

If you would like to explore these ideas further, my book *Tarot and the Magus* is a good starter. But in my experience the flexible approach of Card Counting and Elemental Dignities combined with the Tarot cards is enough. This approach takes us from fixed views on the known into areas that were unexplored. This is the reason why there are hardly any cabbalistic references in this book. The problem with the cabbalistic Tree of Life is its stasis and rigidity.

READING CATHERINE'S UNCOUNTED CARDS

When we start to analyse a spread, we find that some cards and sequences will occur over and over again. As we become more adept at card counting, we start to look for the cards that are ignored by the others. Now is the time to look at the cards that have so far remained hidden from our scrutiny. We will do this for the basic spread, and then for the Queen of Pentacles and for Temperance. We will also consider the differences that counting Aces as eleven makes too.

Basic Spread

There is only one card that is completely uncounted, and it is the Knight of Wands, the very card that Catherine sees as her future. No wonder she is having difficulty seeing him and how he could feature in her life. The Three of Swords, the card of sorrow and loss is uncounted in one direction. These two cards together sum up the situation.

Aces as Eleven

The Three of Swords and the Knight of Wands are unchanged, and into the mix is added the Ace of Cups.

Queen of Pentacles

The Three of Swords is now completely uncounted, as is the Eight of Cups. Several more cards count onto the Knight of Wands. When the Aces count eleven, there is no change to the Three of Swords or the Eight of Cups, but now the Knight of Wands has eight cards counting onto it.

Temperance

The Three of Swords and the Eight of Cups are uncounted, both for Aces as five and as eleven.

Queen of Pentacles and Temperance

There are no uncounted cards.

Summary

If we counted only from the first card, the Eight of Cups, we would have never known its status as an uncounted card. When the cards are laid out for a normal Celtic Cross spread, the Three of Swords would stick out like a sore thumb—I can feel the shudders as the reader turns it over, even though its position in the spread is in the Past. The Eight of Cups is not a very inspiring card either. As you can see, except for the final combination, the status of the uncounted cards hardly changes, at least for this reading.

Catherine's View On The Uncounted Cards

We begin by looking at the cards that were either uncounted or barely touched on. Paul and I created tables to check the counting for all the cards, including the added cards, and the two possible counts with the Ace. While this wouldn't be normal practice, for the purpose of this book it proved useful to check every combination.

With the exception of the last layout, which included the Queen of Pentacles and Temperance together, three particular cards stood out. Amazingly, those cards are also the reversed cards from the original spread: the Eight of Cups, the Three of Swords and the Knight of Wands. Of these, the Three of Swords was the clear winner in receiving the least amount of hits.

So what does that mean? Paul clearly states that he considers uncounted cards to be the origin of the problem or the first step in a new beginning, depending on whether they represent either the past or the future. I have no doubt that in my case the Three of Swords represents my past and my willingness to move forward with a fresh outlook and renewed optimism toward my future.

That still leaves the Eight of Cups and the elusive Knight of Wands. The Eight of Cups I would confidently place with the Three of Swords, but we cannot deny that the Knight is a part of the future for at least two reasons: firstly, because of his placement in the Outcome position in the original Celtic Cross spread; and secondly because I did not actually recognise him as someone in my life.

For a lot of the counting, the Knight of Wands is a frequent visitor to all of the cards in the 'staff' or column part of the Celtic Cross spread, cards which certainly do not pertain to the past. This kind of information wouldn't necessarily be so obvious without the tables we created, but it does at least add weight to the conclusion that this Knight is not from my past. So where do we go now?

First we need to look at those reversed cards again, but this time as a whole. We began our reading by noting we had three reversed cards, and we are ending our reading with those same three reversed cards, only this time we are viewing them from a different perspective. I believe there is significance here and not just coincidence. We have two cards related to the past and one to the future, so how do we tie them together? It is possible that the healing of the past (the Eight and the Three) will come from a future encounter with the Knight. It is also possible that this Knight may well cause fresh pain and loss in the future. So how do we discover the answer?

Paul suggests that the answers may be found with the spirits of the Tarot themselves: the Goetia, or Jinn as some call them. He has vast experience working in this area and talks about them as nonchalantly as he would discuss dinner plans! Not everyone would be happy to be aligned with them, however, and I feel it's important to bring this into the open and discuss it further.

As I've undertaken no direct working in this field, I consider myself unqualified to advise anyone as to whether they should seek out direct spirit contact. What I can say is that I believe we all have contact with the spiritual world every day, whether it is through our dreams or our waking lives.

When we take our own spiritual journeys further, who knows what or who we encounter along the way? Opening ourselves to increased psychic awareness, clairvoyance, or just trying to connect better means that we are stepping into a world different from our physical existence. We are connecting to spirits and the spiritual, only most of us cannot see them, but certainly we can hear them if we choose to listen.

During my own spiritual quest I have begun meditations to connect with my Higher Self. I have seen beings of light and stepped into some strange places, and I have heard my spirit guides as clear as day. Since I have been working with Paul, my dreams are more lucid and—on occasion—prophetic. I have flashes of inspiration so frequently now that even I have begun to question whether they are coming from me!

So what does all this mean and how does it relate to the Knight of Wands? The answer is as simple for me now as it was for Paul all along. Listen to your inner self. Learn to tap in to whatever spiritual force you are comfortable with. That could be the Goetic spirits, it could be your Higher Self, it could be the Angels. It could be that quiet voice you listen to in times of trouble. The point is that the answer often lies within. The method you use to bring it out is up to you.

I have the feeling that some of you may feel cheated because I haven't revealed the identity of the mysterious Knight of Wands. Maybe you feel that the reading or our methods haven't produced the answer, but consider this: the tarot isn't an address book. It is not a scrying device and it certainly hasn't so far produced the winning Lottery numbers for anyone.

The answer to the question comes from listening to that quiet voice, looking out for serendipity and acting on those impulses you cannot always explain. Ask to be shown the answers you seek, record your dreams and flashes of inspiration. And also consider this: do you really want to know all the answers? Wouldn't life get a little dull without some nice surprises along the way?

If you really, really must know who the Knight of Wands is, then you'd better keep reading...

Who Is The Knight Of Wands?

So who is the Knight of Wands? I made a prediction to Catherine early on that the Knight of Wands would appear in late March. We are now at the end of May and he has not turned up. What has gone wrong? As Catherine and I became more absorbed in the writing of this book, his importance receded somewhat. Catherine became more philosophical and she had her own busy life to get on with.

Still, predictions are predictions, and we have to address this point. Did all our work on transforming Catherine's Celtic Cross Spread into a more powerful analytical system lose its focus? Was it all a waste of time? Catherine mentioned in an email who she thought the Knight of Wands might be, but I did not lend the suggestion much credence. However, when I told her the Knight's identity right at the end of writing this book, she was shocked. This was surprising, given that she had been *right* about whom he was originally, and I had merely caught up weeks later!

Even at this late stage in the writing of this book, surprises continue. Is there an end to the number of layers in this cosmic onion? Compared to the finality of the Celtic Cross Spread, the techniques of Card Counting and Elemental Dignities stimulate a process of evolution that works at the material, emotional, psychological and spiritual levels. When Catherine contacted me, her confidence was low in her ability to read the Tarot. As we continued to work on the analysis, it was easy to see how much she was changing. She began to devour as much knowledge as possible on the Tarot, scouring the internet, researching in ever greater depth. Her questions became more pointed and sophisticated. She began to push me into doing something I had wanted to do for ages, but until she came along I had not seen how to move forward. Very quickly, Catherine moved into areas of the Tarot that are very abstract and difficult to describe without direct knowledge. Her spiritual perceptions moved to the point that she began to have contact with the Goetia, a group of spirits considered by many (although not by me, naturally), to be very difficult to work with, something to be attempted only by the most advanced magicians. Catherine, of course, does not consider herself a magician, and I would agree with that. It should be remembered, too, that she and I have corresponded solely through emails.

So, back to the main question. My expertise is with Aleister Crowley's Thoth Tarot, but we have been using the Rider-Waite Tarot throughout this book. For the first time, I decided to pick up the Thoth Tarot to see if there were any answers. At the heart of Catherine's quest was the understanding of the two Knights. As we know, the Knight of Pentacles represents her past, so why is he appearing in the Future position in the Celtic Cross? The Knight of Wands in the Outcome position is reversed, which is not particularly positive, but when we analyse the spread using Card Counting and Elemental Dignities it is clear that the Knight is so completely outside Catherine's circle that he hardly interacts with any of the other cards. True, he does connect in a few places, but there again, the Uncounted Cards, the Eight of Cups and the Three of Swords, make it difficult for Catherine to get beyond loss and feelings of emptiness. Uncharacteristically, the Knight of Wands waits patiently on the periphery, mute. To my mind, the Knight is akin to the Fool, someone so different from Catherine's experience that she cannot recognise him.

Throughout this book the divinatory meanings of the cards have largely been ignored in favour of looking at the *relationships* between them, the flows of energy, and how that energy changes over time. As I read Crowley's description of the two Knights, I saw that they clearly represent the old and the new phases of Catherine's life. Starting with the Knight of Pentacles, Crowley says: 'his function is entirely confined to the production of food'.

The Knight looks after the basics, just as Catherine has been working hard as a single mother, not having the time or the inclination for relationships. We get a glimmer of understanding why he appears as the Outcome; in her heart, Catherine does not expect her role in life to change. Crowley's description of the Knight of Pentacles demonstrates a lack of initiative, a preoccupation with material things; intellectually he is not bright. The fire within is smouldering but it has not caught alight. We need more energy, and the Knight of Wands provides precisely that:

> The moral qualities appropriate to this figure are activity, generosity, fierceness, impetuosity, pride, impulsiveness, swiftness in unpredictable actions.

Crowley's advice is timely:

> ...great emphasis is laid on the startling, perilous, and revolutionary character of the events cognate. The Querent is advised to be apprehensive, yet cool, resolute and energetic: to beware of untimely action, but to go forward with tense confidence in his own ability.

Thus far, we have been considering the Knights as external, but here is a case for considering them as two choices, two phases in Catherine's life. Clearly Catherine is better off with the fire and passion of the Knight of Wands, a man who has awakened something within her, from which she should move forward with confidence.

Looking back at Catherine's original email to me, I note the question she asked: 'Will I find the man of my dreams?' In the light of the spiritual discourse of the previous chapter and the transformations in her dreams, it could well be that the Tarot has answered in the affirmative. Perhaps we should have been looking in the spiritual realms all along, and not for a man of flesh and blood. You have probably guessed by now that I stand outside the family and social circle of Catherine's life. Catherine's life is in the North West of England while I reside on the South Coast. I do not recognise myself in the Knight of Wands: he is someone quick to start things, but lacks the patience to continue with them to completion. It is just as well that he remained external to me throughout our collaboration. The question remains, however: had I been in her dreams all along? Neither of us remembers. Maybe the dreams were stirred when she came to my web site for answers.

Catherine will go forward with newly found confidence in her abilities. She has found new powers within herself that will unfold as time goes on. She will find new love, but it will be because of these new energies from the Knight of Wands, who will be her equal. Will she undertake another Tarot reading? You would have to ask her. What is for sure is that next time she will phrase the question more carefully.

What impresses me most when I have the privilege to share these techniques with a student is the astonishing growth in the student's confidence, coupled with the desire to experiment and to push the boundaries. As we worked together, Catherine's enthusiasm and determination to push those boundaries was a welcome challenge to my own perceptions and knowledge, to the extent that she was setting the agenda and I had to respond. Throughout the time we worked on this reading I was not teaching as such, since Catherine already knew the techniques. What she needed was greater confidence in her abilities as a Tarot Reader, and some direction as to how to use them.

As a result of our collaboration Catherine has become a professional Tarot Reader. Her blog at www.tarotelements.com is particularly inspiring.

Catherine's Vision

While we were finalising this book, Catherine's journey continued. Her visions have been getting stronger and more profound for some time, but even so we had no original intention to include them. However, this vision demonstrates the healing power we can receive from such an experience. The High Priestess has not been part of this Tarot reading, but her appearance represents empowerment: she is an independent, confident woman who intends to go her own way. This is particularly significant in light of Catherine's original question: 'Will I meet the man of my dreams?'

> I found Pegasus and asked him to take me to the High Priestess. She appeared, dancing, and did some kind of hand-dance with—her left to my right. I'd never seen anything quite like it. Then she did the same thing on my head and around my head and shoulders. We danced together for a while, floating, and then she left, although I didn't see her go. The strange thing was that the figures from the cards are transparent, like glass or crystal. The idea behind this is that they don't manifest as belonging to any particular race, making them universal. After I could not see the High Priestess any more I thanked her for her time and left with Pegasus.

> I've no idea what the hand-dancing meant, or even what she was doing on and around my head. It was as though she were tapping buttons on my hand and head, swirling her hand but also touching me. The strange thing is that although I had never seen this before, when we were hand-dancing I matched her move for move. It was almost as if she were programming me, but how would I know what moves she would make? Around the head it felt like she was blessing me. It was like the way priests make the sign of the cross.

Catherine was not a passive observer in the vision; she was there with the High Priestess, interacting. Was the High Priestess simply giving Catherine healing, or was she instructing Catherine in *how* to heal?

It is the nature of visions that answers are not always forthcoming from them at the time they are seen. Months later (November 2008), Catherine found herself returning to the High Priestess. Note how effortlessly she was able to revisit to the vision:

> I did not hang around on the ground as I was quickly drifting upwards and did not stop. I discovered that on another plane, or in a different dimension, I have a whole different life with people who are from this dimension. It was explained to me, that life on that plane did not mirror this one, but the soul or spirit did. I have a different family on that plane, and when I asked about my children in this world I was told I was only a vehicle to bring their souls into existence and ensure they developed into good people. This other child I saw, who is my daughter, looked nothing like me and I was told that she appeared to me as I expected to see her. Even her name was what I chose here and now.
>
> I was told that doing spiritual work in this world increased my energy and strength in the other one too, and that I needed to do this sooner rather than later. I'm not in any danger or suffering from any lack of en-

ergy per se, but it would seem that my whole being (however many there are of me) is ready for the next level and that as I get stronger here, so I will there too. I was also told that we can drain ourselves of energy across these dimensions. By not taking myself to the next level my whole will loose energy and become weaker.

After the meditation, it made me think of 'energy cords'. If I'm connected to myself across many dimensions through what I would think of as essential cords, then I am feeding myself energy or—at the other extreme—taking too much here and causing an imbalance elsewhere. By *creating* energy here, I can replenish or replace what I am draining. Spiritual work is the quickest route no doubt. If there is enough of it, then I can boost my energy across the dimensions. From what I understood today, increasing it significantly will have beneficial effects across the board. It made me think about 'the Princess of Disks' and 'February'. But I know from this exploration today that February is not soon enough.

('February' may also refer to the past, since this was when Catherine contacted me about her Tarot reading. The significance of 'the Princess of Disks' is explored below.)

There was a sense of urgency about this. I also felt that this other dimension was more spiritual than this one. It was pure spirit, but we were still in families and had partners. Yet I think (or at least I was left with a feeling that) it is less physical, or not physical in the sense that we know here. The everyday crap of this world does not exist in that one: bills, cleaning, the rent, etc. I'm not even sure sex exists in that other world either, not in the sense that we know here. I wonder if that is why the spiritual work is so important. If the physical strain on the spirit is so demanding in that dimension from this one, then we are draining ourselves.

After some reflection, Catherine recognised the child:

> I have dreamt of this child before, as a baby, not so long ago. It seems odd she was here again today. She actually came to me and climbed onto me and nestled herself on my lap with her arms around my neck and I did not know who she was until I was told she was my daughter. There is no doubt, though, that she knew me.

I was reminded of the 'Babe in the Abyss' described by Aleister Crowley in the first Enochian Aethyr, LIL. The babe could represent Catherine's Higher Genius.

Compare Crowley's description of the veil hiding LIL in *The Vision and the Voice* with his description of the High Priestess in *The Book of Thoth*:

> The veil of the Aethyr is like the veil of night, dark azure, full of countless stars. And because the veil is infinite, at first one seeth not the winged globe of the sun that burneth in the centre thereof. (*The Vision and the Voice*)

> She is clothed only in the luminous veil of night. It is important for high initiation to regard Light not as the perfect manifestation of the Eternal Spirit, but rather as the veil which hides that Spirit... She is the truth behind the veil of light. She is the soul of light. (*The Book of Thoth*)

The Princess of Disks is the last card in the Tarot deck, so she represents rebirth (the beginning is in the end). Crowley calls her the 'woman on the brink of transformation'.

> The main theme of this, though, was the spiritual work and how important it is, both time-wise and developmentally. Whether I exist on another plane or in a parallel universe remains to be seen; the urgency

was expressed nonetheless. Spiritually, this will develop me. I wondered if it is a way to raise my vibration (as they say), or increase my frequency. Though I know little of this, it is something I have been thinking about for a while. I thought about resonance and vibration down the connecting threads, rather like a spiders web.

A fascinating aspect of Catherine's visions is that at no time did we ever do any pathworking. Nor did we discuss the Cabbalistic Tree of Life, where the High Priestess connects Tiphareth to Kether. Clearly the function of the High Priestess is to connect to 'higher planes' (for want of a better description), and this can easily be done without the framework of the Tree of Life. The Hebrew letter associated with the High Priestess is Gimel, which means 'the camel', who is able to easily traverse vast expanses of the desert bereft of signposts. In *The Book of Thoth*, the High Priestess card is covered by a matrix of filigree representing the geometry of other dimensions. Could it be that the High Priestess represents the spiritual technique and power of Card Counting?

Epilogue

Most Tarot readings last fifteen minutes to half an hour. This is usually time enough to address most of the needs or questions of the client, but when the rapprochement is strong and the client demonstrates the desire for deeper insights, judicious use of the techniques described are pertinent. I use all the techniques to a greater or lesser extent in every Tarot reading. As I have spent so many years using them, analysis is almost unconscious. The purpose is not to portray the Tarot Reader as some kind of God, but rather to enable and empower the client to take control of her life, to empower herself, and to find her own inner direction. Performed in relationship with each other both the Tarot Reader and the Client will grow from the experience.

Questions that begin 'Will I find—?' are no stranger to the Tarot Reader. On the face of it, they sound quite powerful because 'will' can indicate an exercise of will rather than a question. However, the brutal answer is often: 'Not unless you change yourself in some way'. These days, clients want instant gratification and a magical spell to give them what they desire. To answer simply in the affirmative opens the Tarot Reader to the distinct possibility that their prophecy will fail, as the Client sits back and prepares to wait. As this book demonstrates, the questions of *Who?* and *When?* can become subsumed under a fascination with the inner realms. Catherine, however, was able to unpeel the layers of her psyche as it related to her situation.

Tarot Readers who are either suspicious of 'psychic powers' or feel they lack psychic gifts will find comfort in these techniques, as all that is required are the basic skills of counting up to twelve and the simple logic of the four elements. For those who are interested in improving their psychic skills, the comfortable assimilation and regular use of these techniques results in deeper perceptions, as we have seen in Catherine's Vision.

CATHERINE'S FINAL THOUGHTS

On the evening that I first emailed Paul about my reading, I drew a single card to get a feel of what might happen. I wasn't delighted to see the Tower, but I instinctively knew that whatever was going to be cleared away had outstayed its welcome—only something good would be filling the void. This turned out to be the case and in the time I have known Paul, as teacher, mentor and friend, much has been cleared away from my beliefs, my thoughts and my psyche.

Paul hasn't filled me with new beliefs or directed me on any path; he has always just been there to guide me when I needed a hand. If I had questions, he would answer them. Sometimes he wouldn't answer any at all and I would get very frustrated! He did this purely so I would form my own ideas and opinions on the new things I was discovering almost daily—he understood the need to remain impartial so that I would come to my own conclusions and I thank him for that now. Free thinking is a wonderful thing and the Tarot is a terrific partner. All you need to progress is a deck of cards and personal honesty.

The reading that I brought to Paul in February 2008 focused on my love life, but analysing those ten cards turned into a very cathartic process and became a life-changing event; not just the time I spent with Paul, but the changes I made in my life, personally and professionally. I finally had the confidence to become a professional Tarot reader after many years of hiding behind the veil, but— more than that—I found a new love and a new outlet: my Tarot blog, *Tarot Elements*.

Paul encouraged me from very early on to develop an online presence, but I resisted—as Paul would no doubt tell you. It seemed a tall order, building a website; but a close friend introduced me to blogging and I've never looked back. *Tarot Elements* was born in April 2009 and it has since become the creative outlet that I've been seeking for a long time.

The Tower did make a massive impact on my life from that day onwards, and a lot of good has resulted from its effects.

About The Authors

Paul Hughes-Barlow has been reading Tarot professionally for twenty-five years. He is expert in the Opening of the Key Spread, from which the tarot techniques used in this book originate. His first book, *Tarot and the Magus*, explores these techniques from a more magical point of view. Life is fluid, a constant continuum ever unfolding and changing. The methods used in this and his previous book explore the relationships between the cards, which reflect the symbiotic relationship between our inner and outer worlds. His passion has been, and continues to be, assisting his clients to recognize the choices available to them which lie veiled until a reading helps to expose them through the techniques he uses and describes in this book. His website is supertarot.co.uk.

Now a professional Tarot reader and blogger, **Catherine Chapman** can be found every day at her Tarot blog, *Tarot Elements* (tarotelements.com) and aims to share the knowledge she has gained through her time with Paul and by her own explorations and discoveries. She strives to present her work as visually as possible, making it accessible to Tarot readers and students of all levels. Articles range from full Tutorial Series to Tarot Tips and everything in between.

Tarot Elements is a lively blog with a growing number of readers and followers. Catherine actively encourages conversation on her blog and interacts with all her visitors through the comments section on posted articles and on the Guestbook and Wall. You are openly invited to come over to say hello to Catherine at www.tarotelements.com where you will receive a warm welcome and a smile.

www.ingramcontent.com/pod-product-compliance
Ingram Content Group UK Ltd.
Pitfield, Milton Keynes, MK11 3LW, UK
UKHW020857160426
5217IPUK00036B/1628